Love Carved in Stone

Daniel R. Seagren

Regal Books

A Division of GL Publications
Ventura, CA U.S.A.

The foreign language publishing of all Regal books in under the direction of GLINT. GLINT provides financial and technical help for the adaptation, translation and publishing of books for millions of people worldwide. For information regarding translation, contact: GLINT, P.O. Box 6688, Ventura, California 93006.

Scripture quotations in this publication, unless otherwise noted, are from the *Revised Standard Version* of the Bible, copyrighted 1946 and 1952 by the Division of Christian Education of the NCCC, U.S.A., and used by permission.

© Copyright 1983 by Regal Books

Published by Regal Books
A Division of GL Publications
Ventura, California 93006
Printed in U.S.A.

Library of Congress Cataloging in Publication Data

Seagren, Daniel.
    Love carved in stone.

    (Bible commentary for laymen)
    Includes bibliographical references.
    1. Ten commandments. I. Title. II. Series.
BV4655.S445   1983   241.5'2   82-23195
ISBN 0-8307-0840-5

CONTENTS

A Teacher's Manual and Student Discovery Guide for Bible study groups using this book are available from your church supplier.

To Barbara, Laurie and Scott with love.

PREFACE

A certain man climbed a mountain where he stayed longer than expected. After a while his people—for he was their leader—came to the conclusion that he must have disappeared forever. In their grief they decided that a celebration was in order.

Having watched their neighbors for years, undoubtedly with some envy, they borrowed a routine which appeared to have just the right rhythm. Midway through the festivity, their leader unexpectedly appeared. When he saw what they were doing, he became so angry he smashed to the ground the two tablets of stone he was carrying.

Descending the rest of the way, Moses took the newly created center of attraction, a calf fashioned out of gold, ground it into a fine powder and dumped it into the drinking water. Then he made his people drink. A heathen ritual had been unceremoniously upstaged by righteous indignation.

But this was not all. Moses ordered his men to kill anyone who had worshiped this idol. Meanwhile the broken bits of the *Decalogue* cluttered the mountainside.

What an awkward introduction for something as important as the *Decalogue*.

Unfortunately, the Ten Commandments have too often been awkwardly introduced since that momentous event ages ago. As Moses trudged back up the mountain he didn't stop to pick up the pieces. The tablets were demolished, yes, but not the message. God inscribed them once more, and so they remain—unbroken, ageless, terse, exacting, unfathomed, simple. Simple in the sense that a child can understand them; unfathomed in that the wisest sages of all time have not been able to exhaust their meaning. The deeper we probe these eternal etchings, the more indelible they become.

In no way should this book be considered an exhaustive, all-inclusive treatment of the Ten Commandments. Rather, consider it as a means of finding solid ground on which to build not only the human race but the individual family. For those wishing to study the deeper implications of the Decalogue, there are many excellent books available. This author, however, has deliberately limited the study to the family and everyday living and it should be understood in this context.

The family of today is in trouble. Civilizations have come and gone; some realized, often too late, that the family was its underlying curse or blessing. The preservation of the family has always been in jeopardy. In this study we shall probe into the family, using the two-edged sword of the Decalogue. God has allowed us to discover scientific laws by trial and error, but He never intended that we should unravel the mysteries of ethical precepts and moral laws by chance. The highest moral and ethical order of the universe must be revealed.

Mankind cannot experiment with humanity as it does with inanimate objects and animals. Varying schools of thought have tried to arrive at a consensus but have been unable to do so. Sociologists, psychologists, scientists and even theologians have been unable to establish a satisfactory ethical system for the human family; textbooks are often outdated before the ink is dry. Theories are discarded, often reluctantly, even when time proves them wrong.

Because of this, God has revealed a *blueprint* by which the human family can build its home. Building a home today is both exciting and dangerous; without a plan it is disastrous. Therefore, in the following pages we will attempt to give encouragement as well as instruction to those who stand in need of a sure foundation—and that is most of us.

Since there is some confusion regarding the numerical

sequence of the Ten Commandments, let me briefly explain the sequence we will follow in this study. Basically, there are three traditional options: (1) the first and second commandments are combined and the tenth is divided into two parts; (2) (the one used in this study) separates the commandments according to *priority* (first) and *superiority* (second); (3) the order of the commandments dealing with murder (sixth) and adultery (seventh) are reversed, following the Greek version of the Old Testament.

For some this is a matter of personal preference; for many it is a matter of tradition; for others it is a theological or historical perspective. For me, personally, it is a combination of these. In childhood I learned the Decalogue in the sequence followed by this study. Since those days, certain insights and convictions have reinforced this numerical order. These will be reflected as the study progresses.

Incidentally, a mention could be made of another alternative: (4) nine commandments. This results when the first and second commandments are combined or two commands are not made from the tenth. Rarely, if ever, is this sequence suggested as an alternative.

With this in mind it is my hope that no one will be distressed by the sequence followed in this study because the material will be relevant regardless of your position. So that you may readily focus your attention on the order in which the Ten Commandments will be presented, the following short form is given below:

   I.   You shall have no other gods before me.
  II.   You shall not make for yourself any graven image.
 III.   You shall not take the name of God lightly.
 IV.   Remember the sabbath day, to keep it holy.
  V.   Honor your father and mother.
 VI.   You shall not kill.
 VII.   You shall not commit adultery.
VIII.   You shall not steal.
 IX.   You shall not bear false witness.
  X.   You shall not covet.

INTRODUCTION

Centuries before Christ was born, Moses introduced the Decalogue to the Hebrew people. Since then it has been rewritten, rephrased, abbreviated, expanded, distorted, maligned, ignored, and underestimated.

Today, whenever we violate one of God's laws, natural or moral, *we* are broken, not the law itself. Individuals, families, nations, and civilizations have destroyed themselves as God's eternal law is neglected or rejected.

We who live in the twentieth century tend to believe that the Decalogue was a masterful document in its era: a concise, direct, and sensible code of ethics for a much more primitive people. However, the Ten Commandments are no longer adequate, since we have come of age; in a very real sense, we say, we have outgrown the Decalogue.

We who think this way often do not throw out moral ideals inspired by the ancient scribes, but we prefer not to become bound by the so-called obsolete etchings. Rather, the Sermon on the Mount and the Golden Rule show the way. This is unfortunate. Our thesis is simple: we need both the Decalogue *and* the Beatitudes, law *and* grace, Moses *and* Jesus, the Old *and*

New Testaments.

Matthew clearly demonstrates the relationship between the Decalogue and the teachings of Jesus:

> One of them, a lawyer, asked him a question, to test him. "Teacher, which is the great commandment in the law?" And he said to him, "You shall love the Lord your God with all your heart, and with all your soul, and with all your mind. This is the great and first commandment. And a second is like it, You shall love your neighbor as yourself. On these two commandments depend all the law and the prophets" (Matt. 22:35-40).

The lawyer was trying to trap Jesus with a loaded question. The Master simply answered that the law has two major aspects. The first aspect is the *vertical* relationship between God and man. The first four commandments of the Decalogue were summed up beautifully by the Lord in His answer: You shall love the Lord your God with all your heart, soul, and mind. The second aspect covers the last six commandments that deal with *horizontal* relationships—person to person. Jesus wrapped this up with even more brevity: You shall love your neighbor as yourself.

But how does the law fit the picture?

> Think not that I have come to abolish the law and the prophets; I have come not to abolish them but to fulfil them . . . . Whoever then relaxes one of the least of these commandments and teaches men so shall be called least in the kingdom of heaven; but he who does them and teaches them shall be called great in the kingdom of heaven. For I tell you, unless your righteousness exceeds that of the scribes and Pharisees, you will never enter the kingdom of heaven (Matt. 5:17-20).

In this and numerous other passages Jesus shows the close relationship between the law and the gospel.

Since there are many misunderstandings regarding the law in general, and the Decalogue in particular, let us probe into some of the prevailing sentiments.

WE LIVE UNDER GRACE, NOT LAW

This is a most understandable, and often valid, objection. It stems primarily from our understanding of the term *law*. Laws can be miserable impositions placed on a society. All of us have felt the sting of unjust or meaningless laws.

Still, we could not possibly exist without law and order. Certain laws are necessary simply because we cannot read minds. On the highway, for instance, laws are necessary not only because drivers are greedy but also because a person wouldn't know whether he should *zig* or *zag* when meeting an oncoming car. Certain drivers may slow down when school lets out but laws have been enacted to make certain that we do.

I once saw an attractive pamphlet with this title: "A GIRL MAY MARRY AT ANY AGE WITH HER PARENTS' CONSENT. RIGHT? WRONG!!! HERE'S WHY. . . . " This led the reader into a booklet which began, "There's a law . . . " In short, it stated that a society can and often must go beyond the jurisdiction of parents. In this case, a fifteen-year-old girl may not legally get married, with or without parental consent. When she is sixteen she may apply for a license, but will be permitted to marry only with the consent of both parents, or one parent, or a guardian having custody, plus the consent of the judge or the juvenile court of the county where the girl resides. Why?

At times parents are irresponsible people and consequently irresponsible parents. The daughter of a friend of mine was molested. The molester had a bad record and was already a menace to society. The father pressed charges. Later, he was talked into dropping charges by a clergyman who believed he was getting through to the delinquent. However, when it came to court, the judge refused to allow the father to drop charges. Unfair? The father had jurisdiction over the daughter, yes, but the judge was responsible for the entire community. A hoodlum like this, he implied, endangered the lives of other young girls. The prosecution went on.

When we understand that there are bad laws, good laws, redundant laws, inadequate laws, complex laws, and naive laws, we begin to understand that the era of grace cannot and should not outlaw either maxims or jurisprudence. Laws are essential in an ordered society whether in the home or courtroom or on the highway. Grace and law are not incompatible.

LAWS SHOULD BE TEACHERS, NOT TRUANT OFFICERS

We object to police brutality. We do not object to a well-trained, disciplined policeman getting tough when the situation warrants it. We abhor the father who mercilessly beats his children. At the same time we shudder when we see parents destroy their offspring by condoning everything they do. When a reckless, carefree Yankee hot-rods it through King Arthur country we expect English laws to stiffen. And when a hostile, belligerent chap takes over a classroom we expect the teacher to take necessary action in order that the rest of the class might learn.

Basically, the objection to the law-enforcer is getting at something important. Too often, persons in authority take on ugly dispositions. A child in charge of a street crossing can allow authority to go to his head. Employers can lord over hapless employees. A coach can become tyrannical, a husband can be unduly miserly as he chokes off the household budget, an older sister can breed contempt as she stretches her prerogatives, etc.

In these instances, and a host of others equally contemptible, the orders executed may have been sound but the command, law, rule, order becomes intolerable because of the one who administered it. We must be careful not to lose respect for law and order, maxims and dictums simply because we have lost respect for the executor. Laws can teach and should be administered in a spirit of understanding and respect. Exceptions at times are necessary but should never become the rule.

When Johnny is expected to wash the family car on a weekly basis, he should not be driven, intimidated, cajoled, or even bribed to fulfill his rightful share of family responsibility. He is expected to keep the family car clean because he is a member of the family. The reason why he is to do this must be explained to him carefully and firmly (and early in life). Johnny will then know why he must fulfill this obligation. The skill with which parents are able to inspire children to act as responsible members of the family varies considerably. Laws can teach, and at times teaching seems to be a thankless task. But teach we must.

LAWS ONLY LEAD TO LEGALISM

Somehow I cannot forget the story of the youngster who, when asked, refused to sit down. He was asked again more sternly. Again he refused. Finally, with no polite ceremony he was shoved down into the chair where he sat, yet not without the last word: "I may be sitting down, but I'm standing up inside." It still holds true: *A man convinced against his will is of the same opinion still*.

There is no need to argue that laws can lead to legalism. Where we must argue is obvious: all laws need not lead to legalism. When I drive on the left side of the highway in England, it is not because I am legalistic or because I fear a head-on collision, but because it is the rational thing to do. If I see another car in my lane I move over, not because I have to but because I want to. I'll avoid an accident at almost any cost.

Back again to Johnny and the washing of the family buggy. If he is compelled to wash the family set of wheels without understanding that this is his rightful share as a responsible member of the family, he no doubt will wash it legalistically (or at least until a clean car is to his personal advantage). Unfortunately, we too often make our structured society a world of meaningless prohibitions and mandates. Then laws are merely legalistic.

THE DECALOGUE IS ADEQUATE FOR A PRIMITIVE SOCIETY

As we shall see, the Ten Commandments have hardly been exhausted in several thousand years of usage. The wiser the person, the more studious, the greater is the magnitude of the

Decalogue. Today many people understand the tablets of stone in much the same way the Hebrews did. They knew the sixth command said not to kill. They also knew the distinction between killing and murder.

Let's look at this command for a moment: *Thou shall not kill*. This is clear enough, especially when we interpret killing as murder. However, we need all of Scripture plus the wisdom of Solomon to get meaningful answers on troublesome areas associated with this command—abortion, euthanasia (mercy killing), accidental homicide, capital punishment, suicide, self-defense and war.

As we probe more deeply into the Decalogue we must come to grips with attitudes, motives, and circumstances. We soon discover that we are a special creation, endowed by the Creator with an eternal soul with the capacity to worship and the ability to deal with abstractions; in short, we are made in the likeness of God. Consequently, God has made an indelible mandate: do not tamper with my creation. People are sacred.

We must be careful not to indict the ancient Hebrews as primitives. We have yet to exhaust or even improve on many of the teachings and practices of these people. This does not mean that there has been no upward spiraling. It simply means that the Decalogue was extremely meaningful to them and is equally challenging to us. It also means that we must differentiate between universal laws and tribal commands.

There are civil, moral, and ceremonial laws inherent within every tribe and nation. The Ten Commandments, as interpreted in this study, transcend all tribal laws and societal mores. Other studies may deal more closely with these lesser distinctions; we will adhere to the basic ten.

BUT WHY ARE THEY ALL SO NEGATIVE?

Eighty percent of the Decalogue is written in the negative. This is an unfortunate hurdle that the law must leap. The animosity felt toward the Decalogue because it is expressed in the negative is no doubt considerable. Exactly why Jehovah etched them this way is uncertain. Many reasons have been given;

some seem to be less than persuasive. Let me simply give two homey illustrations that may throw some light on the subject.

When my son was an energetic three-year-old, he had a "burning" desire to help his dad (sometimes this desire seems to diminish with age). One day he was standing by me as I placed another log on the fire. Out of the corner of my eye I saw him moving toward the fire to push the logs into a better position. Whirling around, I yelled, "Look out!" and instinctively pulled him back. Sure, he knew the fire was hot, but all he could think about was the log that hadn't settled quite right. All I could think about was the potential danger. My negative shout was love and fear all wrapped into one. I wasn't scolding. I wasn't about to wait for the outcome (to see if he would reach into the fire or not). I didn't think in terms of negative or positive. I had only one thought: I didn't want Scott to get burned! It was that simple. I used language and tone of voice he could understand.

A number of years ago, when I was about the same age as my son just mentioned, our family visited Niagara Falls. My father, suddenly realizing that I was missing, looked frantically for me. Knowing my temperament and daring he suspected the worst. Turning toward the river he spotted me right at the edge of a wall high above the roaring falls. Somehow I had climbed through a fence and had wandered onto this precarious perch. Dad did not yell at me. Instead he turned and began walking away, simply calling in a calm voice, "Daniel, we are going now." In a few moments I left the dangerous edge and soon caught up with the family. The crisis was over.

Crisis? My father knew me. He was reasonably sure that if he yelled at me I might take it as a challenge to play games, and in that perilous position I might have bolted into the Niagara. His wisdom may have saved my life.

Here we have two illustrations. In one, a negative command was used; in the other, a positive. Both came from fathers who deeply loved their sons. When our heavenly Father inscribed these principles for His sons, He acted out of a father's love for His children, using language we can understand. When God said, *Do not steal* and *Do remember the Sabbath*, the point is well established. Although we may not fully understand the negative and positive wording, the implications often drive us deeper than many of us want to go.

WHY ARE MORAL LAWS REVEALED WHEN NATURAL LAWS ARE DISCOVERED?

This is a significant question. God evidently was taking no chances on humankind being able to discover principles underlying ideal behavior. In the natural world we are free to experiment, test hypotheses, and draw conclusions. God will not allow mankind to discover eternal principles using the scientific method. This is one reason the eternal Architect revealed the moral law. On the other hand, we do well to remember that throughout the entire Bible there are innumerable hints and outright statements showing us that God has revealed some natural laws as well.

Ignaz Philipp Semmelweis, born in 1818, was eventually driven to insanity because his colleagues in medicine would not be convinced that disease could be transmitted from one patient to another. When *The Cry and the Covenant* advocated the simple idea that doctors wash their hands under running water instead of in a germ-laden basin, they scoffed at him. He argued unsuccessfully that this would reduce the high death rate due to cadaveral contagion and puerperal fever. This procedure, along with other amazing insights into physical health, is given in the ancient book of Leviticus.

Many other biblical hints have led scientists into fruitful discoveries. The Scriptures long ago compared the stars of the sky to the sands of the sea which was not verified until rather recently. The infinite wisdom of Jehovah has literally inundated us with scientific insights; the God of the Hebrews was not only concerned with moral law. Still, we often prefer to disregard the divine blueprint and trudge along, doing exactly what God intended that we should not do. By trial and error, controlled experimentation, scientific calculation (computerized and all), we keep on accepting, modifying, and disregarding human theories. Especially is it tragic when these theories involve human behavior and ethical matters. This is why God has revealed the moral and ethical laws of the universe which are condensed into the ageless Decalogue.

THE DECALOGUE IS JUST TOO SIMPLE

At best, the Decalogue is a paradox. Even though it states ten important principles, these precepts are expanded in Scripture as well as in other religious works, until there are countless laws, precepts, maxims, axioms and elaborations on the ten, involving civil, moral and ceremonial dimensions. Only a divine economy of words can explain the simplicity of the Decalogue. But with the addition of innumerable subsidiary commands, explanations, elaborations and conditions, suddenly the simple becomes complex.

This decalogical simplification is purposeful, but it is hardly oversimplification. God has purposefully kept the heart of the moral law concise. At the same time, all Scripture cries out to be considered in the ultimate understanding of the Decalogue.

MAN CANNOT POSSIBLY KEEP THE LAW

Many fail to keep the law not because the challenge is too great but because it isn't great enough. We've been told that if we aim at nothing we can't miss. How many have been lost to Christianity not because the demands were beyond reach but because the lost were bored, unimpressed, understimulated, unchallenged? A motivated person, upon solving a problem, reaches out for another.

The Decalogue outlines the kind of life worth living and the kind of family worth talking about; it also dares us to try God's way. After purchasing some item which needs to be put together and spending a miserable hour or two trying to figure it out, we finally look at the instruction sheet and see in small print this message: "When all else fails, read the directions." We tend to try our own way, turning to the directions only when all else fails.

Only one person has been able to measure up to the expectations of the law. Jesus came into the world primarily to die in order that we might live, but He has also given us an example of what it is to live the exemplary life—the life worth living. Although it is true that we cannot possibly live up to the law, by God's grace we can move in that direction. Apart from the Decalogue, man is never sure of himself. God's ideal for human existence still presents a vigorous challenge even in the fourth quarter of the twentieth century.

BUT SO MANY LAWS ARE SUB-CHRISTIAN

The Old Testament fairly abounds with laws—laws of every imaginable description, governing every aspect of man's life. No contemporary society would choose to live under that system, nor would moderns try to keep many of those laws.

Every law in the Bible must be surveyed in the light of the Decalogue and in the teaching of Jesus Christ. Because of their hardness of heart, their failure to live by the spirit of the law, and their inability to follow God-given principles, the Hebrew people needed laws to help them maintain the Decalogue. Some of these laws appear to be inferior, perhaps even contradictory. However, when we realize what God, Moses, David, and Josiah were up against, we see that severity and minutia were often mandatory. It was the only kind of language some people would understand.

The same is true today. When parents contribute to the delinquency of a child, the law must get tough. When students on a campus overstep their bounds, specific laws must be laid down. When God said that murder is evil He was also saying that human life is sacred. The eye-for-an-eye concept was instituted, not in contradiction to the sixth commandment, but because there was no other way it could work. Besides, it also served as a restraint: a life could not be taken for a limb.

As the multitude of laws are closely examined in the Old Testament, one dominant message emerges: the laws are God's provision for human benevolence; they are not a tirade against human dignity and common decency. Even laws regarding what a Hebrew could eat and what he could not eat are not picayunish prohibitions depriving the people of tasty morsels. Rather, they were (and are) ingenious insights into food safe to eat and otherwise. Certain meats, for example, may be good eating but almost impossible to preserve for any length of time. The book of Leviticus would make an excellent survival manual. Because of the lack of knowledge, and because of the hardness of man's heart, a multitude of laws were laid down. Properly understood, they are hardly sub-Christian. Properly evaluated, they are not all relevant today.

SITUATIONAL ETHICS HAS REPLACED THE LAW

Situational ethics has always been necessary. Ever since the time of Adam and Eve we have had to make moral decisions. Every situation is unique and must be handled accordingly. A physician is often forced into making precarious moral decisions; a starving man may have to decide between the value of human life versus property. Life is fraught with nerve-wracking decision making.

Applying ethics in diverse situations is demanding. We must act out of human compassion (love) for our neighbor. Yet, one of the greatest difficulties is that the burden placed upon the individual is often far greater than he can bear. We cannot make intelligent decisions without some basic principles to guide our thinking. Even here we may have to choose between two or more principles. A starving man must decide if he should willfully die or steal; a young man may or may not be able to decide if he can serve his country in war. We simply do not have the experience, wisdom, or intelligence to handle every situation without outside assistance. Whenever we live by a series of absolute principles we will not escape situations demanding an ethical decision, but at least we are not expected to make judgments based entirely on our own experience or emotion. The Decalogue does not slam the door of decision making—it provides a hinge on which the door may swing.

A situational ethic which negates all absolutes is dangerous. An ethic based primarily on love fails to understand love.

It has no full understanding of *agape* and relies too heavily upon a curious blend of brotherly and erotic love. The best situational ethic is built upon the absolutes delineated so clearly in the Ten Commandments. No other foundation will suffice.

The Decalogue does not do away with intelligent, sympathetic, compassionate decision making, nor does it demand an insensitive, ruthless, harsh, unbending allegiance. It is given for us to build upon; the sands of time never make good foundations. Situation ethics without eternal principles will bankrupt the family, and along with it, the human race.

Jesus made it very clear that He not only acknowledged the existence of the Decalogue, He stressed its continuing relevance. Christianity, including the structure of the family, needs guidelines. Although we live in an era when rigid standards are abhorred by many, rigid standards are imperative. If the Ten Commandments are viewed as absolute standards for Christians and non-Christians alike (since they are universal principles), this standard for building a home and a society is universal. If these ten principles are developed to their fullest, their wisdom is even more impressive and productive. Hopefully it will make sense for you to build following such a blueprint as the Decalogue. Even though the Ten Commandments were not written specifically for the family, the ten basic principles, if applied by the family, will provide a believable base on which to build not only tribes and nations but families and civilizations.

FOR STUDY OR DISCUSSION

1. Before the Ten Commandments were etched in stone, how did people know what was right or wrong, good or evil?
2. Is it possible to live under grace without some understanding of the law? How?
3. Can you think of an instance when authorities had to take action because of an irresponsible parent or parents?
4. Do you agree: *A man convinced against his will is of the*

same opinion still? Can you think of an example?

5. How would you respond to this statement? "I believe that the Ten Commandments are outmoded."

6. Try to improve on the order of the Ten Commandments.

7. Try putting the negative into the positive and the positive into the negative.

8. Is it ever lawful to break one commandment to save another? (For instance, should a person steal to keep from starving or lie to keep someone from being killed?)

9. Is it wise for a Christian to avoid jobs in which bearing arms or engaging in espionage is necessary?

10. How is it possible for a single parent to effectively teach a child or children in the way he or she ought to go?

Chapter One
PRIORITY

You shall have no other gods before me
Exodus 20:3

Seek first his kingdom and
his righteousness, and all
these things shall be yours as
well (Matt. 6:33).

Arnie was a mediocre student with high ambitions. He
wanted to become a physician, possibly a specialist, some day.
During his earlier college days he fooled around more than he
should have. This gave him only fair grades. Midway through
his third year of college he began to take his studies seriously.
Too seriously. By this time, however, his scholarship was lax
and it took an extremely well-disciplined effort to overcome
his poor study habits. Gradually his grades inched upward,
approaching the minimal mark established by medical schools.
As he neared graduation he had almost made it; another good
quarter might have put him within the mercies of the desired
medical institutions.

Arnie submitted his application to several schools and
began the waiting game. Days trudged by slowly. Finally the
word came. *Sorry . . . We are keeping your name on file, but
. . . We regret to inform you that although your grades have
shown a remarkable improvement during the past year . . .*
When the last letter arrived Arnie didn't bother to open it.
When they found him it was too late.

Betty was a beautiful girl. One day she took all her possessions and headed west. If she would make herself available, she felt she would be discovered. She found plenty of companionship, even some who claimed to have excellent connections. Before many days she realized that the price demanded for services rendered was higher than she imagined. In an unbelievably short time Betty found herself trapped. Although she never got what she had hoped to get, she was in too deeply. She quit struggling and gave in.

Conrad graduated from seminary with honors. Somewhere during his ministry God died. Attempting to help a parishioner with troubles far greater than his own, Conrad soon realized there was little he could offer. His God was dead; his Bible consumed by dust. All he had was himself. Almost before he knew what he was doing, he had sacrificed his lovely family in order to bring temporary happiness to a lonely, passionate parishioner.

Darlene married a handsome brute, intending to overhaul him after the wedding. Discovering that she was unable to make much of a dent on his character, she began to nag. Her unholy nagging only made him more stubborn. As the family grew, tension mounted. After awhile Darlene quit nagging and tried simply to be a good wife and mother. Still nothing happened. Her husband loitered more and more on the way home from work. Household allocations mysteriously disappeared. Darlene finally went to work, not as much out of economic necessity but to get out of the house. Her lovely personality faded; motherly duties and her wifely role became a chore as her mechanical life drifted on and on.

Cases like these are not rare. Each of these individuals was a believer, yet each was unable to cope. Why?

About one out of three marriages is unsuccessful, as are many second marriages. This raw statistic no longer has the capacity to shock. When so many marriages are plagued with some kind of separation (legal or mutual), when countless desertions occur annually, when a large number of the remaining homes have all kinds of internal distress which sometimes does not show externally, we have the right to be sobered.

Murder is often committed against a fellow member of the family. Suicides are not infrequent among teenagers. Delinquents, dropouts, rebels, drug freaks and runaways all reflect unhappy childhoods. Excessive reliance on drugs and youthful appetites for nicotine, alcohol and sex often reflect a family disorder somewhere.

It does not take an expert to realize that the family is in trouble. We hear it everywhere we turn. Invaluable help is coming from many agencies—private, state and national. Marriage clinics and counselors are meeting the problem head-on. Clergymen are bending over backward to save families. Universities are continually experimenting, hiring experts, establishing curricula and conducting extensive research to help combat this malady. Judges and law enforcement officials are concerned; judges are getting tougher or more lenient in order to help remedy the mushrooming problems. Caseworkers are trying to get at the roots of the problems rather than merely treat the symptoms (which is far easier). Even so, much of what we are doing is rehabilitative rather than preventative. Clinics on the family are held in schools and churches; PTAs are concerned, principals are pleading with parents to help maintain discipline. Television stations are airing public service programs with the family in mind. During the evening, parents are asked via TV if they know where their children are. It would be remiss to say that our society is unconcerned, but so many parents either do not know what is happening or have given up.

Attempting to get at the root of family distress, we must offer a strategy that we know works. Authorities are rethinking many of the prevailing theories about the upbringing of children, husband-wife relationships, and who is responsible for the aged. The concept of excessive permissiveness is being reevaluated. Many young parents, the result of overly permissive environments, are rediscovering the hickory stick. There is more knowledge today than ever before on the subject of the family and much of it is valuable. If we could only segregate reliable data from the unreliable and synthesize it into a meaningful philosophy we would do the family an invaluable service. This is where the Ten Commandments come in.

The Ten Commandments were not specifically issued to the family units but given to twelve wayward tribes which needed help badly. The truth found in the Decalogue is universal, not provincial—but it must pass from the family to the tribe to the nation before it can conquer civilization. This author knows the awesome scope of the Mount Sinai "thunderstorms" (Joy Davidman's apt expression) but has applied them to the family, the single parent, and to the extended family where applicable. (We in the U.S.A. live primarily with the so-called nuclear family—parents and children.)

You probably detected the thread which runs through all four cases just mentioned. In each situation, the person involved crumbled when his or her hope was gone. Arnie took his own life when medical school slammed the door. Betty tried to break into the bright lights but was blinded by the awful glare. Conrad fell for the charms of a passionate woman in distress and Darlene couldn't overhaul her man, settling for a miserable half-existence.

These tragedies are not unreal. Arnie could have been that nice kid up the street, your former paperboy. Betty might have been a vivacious cheerleader. Conrad could have served that charming church on Thirty-third, near Hibiscus Hollow. Darlene lives next door (or just around the corner).

What went wrong?

There was nothing dominating their lives that was stronger than they were. We all manage to do quite well when things are going well. Sometimes we are able to take a rough tumble or two, but come apart when we trip too many times. Every person, every family needs something or someone upon whom they can lean. A financial reverse (or too much money), a lingering illness, a devastating problem, a bitter disappointment, a child with a mediocre report card . . . can strike the family at any moment.

This is why the Decalogue begins as it does. It tells us that nothing, absolutely nothing, should come between us and our

God. *You should have no other gods before me*. This is no idle threat; it is a merciful Father who knows that life can get too rough, too complicated for His children.

This first commandment not only sets the tone for the ten, it is also the starting place. When God is given highest priority in the life of an individual, a family, or society itself, other priorities fall into place.

Prior to Moses this principle was written on the heart and orally passed on from one generation to the next. When language was put into writing, it is understandable that God would write His message, too. He wrote not only for Moses and the Hebrews but for all peoples everywhere.

At the time of Moses, idolatry existed everywhere. It was subtle and blatant, merciful and merciless. Idols were hewn out of stone and poured into molds. Idolatry was ascribed to slithering snakes and soaring birds. Idols were movable and stationary, grotesque and stunning.

In the midst of this paganism existed a tribe of people who knew better. The Hebrews had been worshiping the true and living God for countless generations. They knew Him by name and worshiped Him in spirit and truth. Even so, they were human. They had observed exotic pagan pageantry and obscene rituals. They intermingled with their idolatrous neighbors and even intermarried. They were reluctant to discard their own deity and rituals choosing rather to assimilate heathen practices into their own.

It is at this juncture in Hebrew life that Jehovah called Moses to the top of Mount Sinai and boomed forth the Ten Commandments. The first boom was the loudest: YOU SHALL HAVE NO OTHER GODS BEFORE ME. In the tabernacle of the Almighty there is no room for Jehovah and Baal—it's either Jehovah or nothing.

In our twentieth-century life we find it rather incongruous to think of carved idols or anthropomorphic deities. We would never stoop to pay homage to a serpent or doff our cap to a soaring eagle. Yet we usually worship only when it's convenient. We thank God for good health but curse Him when illness strikes. We put "In God We Trust" on our coins but lean on our savings. We eat and drink too much because we forget that our bodies are temples of the Holy Spirit. We say that God is our highest priority but weasel in maintaining His sanctuary. We forget to pray when the sun shines but panic when a storm hits. We send our children to prep schools but not Bible camp. This in part is what God and Moses were talking about. Whatever gets top priority instead of God and spiritual matters is a direct violation of this axiomatic principle better known as the first commandment. Put another way, everything that really matters will be ours if God and what He stands for are given top priority.

A god is an idol, a something or someone that becomes most important in our lives. It could be a dream, a belief, a position, a reputation, a bank account. Whatever or whoever it is that comes first in our life competes with the Almighty for top priority. When God must share the ultimate place with something else, His influence is impaired or nullified. God will not force His way into the center of our existence, but He has let us know that we take an awful chance when we shove Him out of first place. It is dreadfully easy to let mundane, even important things, overly crowd our lives. Before we know it, a shift in the balance of power has occurred and God is no longer able to do for us what He would like to do.

There is an underlying principle here that the secular mind will not argue. He will agree that every person must have some unifying force in his life; he will not agree, however, what this force ought to be. The Judeo-Christian faith claims that God ought to be this unifying force; some secular minds might agree. We also feel that religion (which we often equate with God erroneously) is merely one of several possible unifying forces, which is true. Here is where the great difference lies. Christendom knows that many things will occur that are simply too great for humans to cope with, no matter what the unifying force may be, unless God is allowed to be this central power.

Many actually live rather noble lives without God or religion. They establish a code of conduct and find inspiration in places other than in the church, the Scriptures, or direct communion with the Creator of the universe. More than that, many seculars are better neighbors or partners than some Christians; they often excel in ethical dealings, and many times are more mature and less bigoted. In fact, all of us have seen rather ugly Christians and attractive non-believers living on the same block, but we have also seen some fine believers and ugly non-believers living side by side, too.

The awesome difference is this: both, sooner or later, must deal with the ultimate in life. This includes the reason for our existence, death, life after death, guilt, sin, and evil. Secular man can build an excellent bridge in life, but the bridge is from temporal to temporal. *Man can live by bread alone*—for awhile—but he will not have the strength to make the long journey from here to eternity on his own ingenuity, nor can he help others along the way. Our inner strength may take us through the worst which life can throw at us, but it cannot bridge the gulf between us and God. God is concerned that we have a goal—an ultimate goal—in life and a way of attaining it. The only way this is possible is to make God number one priority in our lives and in our families.

Jesus summarized this command in the classical sentence found in the Sermon on the Mount: *Seek first God's kingdom, and all these things shall be yours as well*. Putting it another way—when God gets top priority in our life, our family, our world, everything else will fall into its proper place.

Although this commandment stresses the necessity of God's priority in our lives—*you shall have no other gods* (priorities) *before me*—it seems wise at this point to think for a moment about priorities.

In our families how does God get top billing? It is at this point where we possibly err without realizing it. At times we place God on a pedestal for our children to see and admire. We hang pictures on our walls, place Bibles in strategic places, subscribe to a Christian journal or two, and say grace at mealtime (and bedtime when the children are small). We even go one step further and make Sunday a day of reverence (or at least of church going) and occasionally invite the pastor or Sunday School teacher home for dinner. We may even indulge in the luxury of family devotions.

As a child, before I could read with any fluency, I remember with pleasure standing behind my father and reading all the insertions placed into the devotional reading for the day (this included references to biblical passages, authors cited, cross references, etc.). These biblical aids were no doubt scholarly, but far removed from the world where children play, fight, struggle, and laugh. But at least I was allowed to be involved. I'm quite sure my family, particularly my father, was not overjoyed with my emerging verbal skills, but to his credit he tolerated it which made it easier for me to tolerate the adult ritual passed off as family devotions.

Giving God (and godliness) top priority in our family affairs cannot be successfully accomplished by reading five hundred solemn words or hanging an appropriate symbol in the vestibule. It must go beyond this or we'll repeat the disastrous fate of the Arnies, Bettys, Conrads and Darlenes of our homes.

Everything we do must involve the Almighty—choosing a career, decision making, planning vacations, changing jobs, purchasing a home, selling a car, attending PTA, or running for a slot on the city council. It is not enough to give God high priority on Sunday morning by rousing a sleepy family into a quickie breakfast before Sunday School (or a low priority by not going fishing because the weather looks forbidding). The Lord's Day can and does become anathema to many because the other days have little or nothing to do with the Lord (except possibly at grace time). Why shouldn't it be somewhat disturbing to have the Almighty invade the only day when the alarm clock could be ignored?

Somehow, somewhere, someone must make it emphatic that God is not an add-on. When He permeates every aspect of our lives, our plans, our hopes, dreams, careers, vacations, and those times of stress and strain, we'll soon discover that He is not a meddlesome person to have around but an indispensable and a very welcome presence. Otherwise God (and His plan for our lives) gets only a low to medium priority so that, when He is needed most, He's likely to have gone fishing (or where does God go when He's really not wanted or needed?).

Maybe the ancient writer wasn't too far off when he said: *Trust in the Lord with all your strength and don't lean too much on your own understanding. Acknowledge him (night and day) and he'll direct your ways* (paraphrased, Prov. 3:5,6). The *RSV* is even more explicit: *Do not rely on your own insight*.

This same kind of divine saturation was made indelible (except that it has faded with time) by Moses who talked about the finger of God etching the commandments in stone. This great prophet said, in part, to his people that they were a people holy to the Lord their God. Because God loved them, He has promised to bless those who love Him and follow His commands, to a thousand generations. To make sure these subsequent generations, including ours, understand this, Moses urged his families to impress this upon their children *when you are sitting in your house, when you are walking by the way, and when you lie down, and when you rise. And you shall write them upon the doorposts of your house and upon your gates* (Deut. 11:19,20; read chapters 9-11).

God never intended that we seek Him Sundays and Wednesdays, at mealtime, or when the chips are falling. Or when we are blessed. In effect He is saying, *Keep me front and center at all times*. Anything short of this is taking a risk, the same risk that has proven disastrous to persons, families, nations, and civilizations.

FOR STUDY OR DISCUSSION

1. What did Arnie, Betty, Conrad and Darlene have in common?
2. How "stubborn" should spouses be in setting priorities?
3. Explain the difference between "preventative" and "rehabilitative" approaches to life (home, school, church, community).
4. Is this statement true: Every parent (couple or single parent) needs someone to lean upon? Who could this

person or those persons be? Is it possible to lean on the wrong person? How?

5. What is the primary unifying force in your life?

6. We all know that some non-Christian neighbors and parents are excellent people, even when compared to Christians. How do we handle this? Do we ever compare weak Christian parents with strong non-Christian parents? What is wrong with this?

7. Must everyone sooner or later deal with the ultimate in life?

8. How can we give God top billing in our family situation?

9. What is indicated when we sit through a ball game in the rain but do not go to church because of the weather?

10. How can YOU make the Lord's Day a meaningful day?

Chapter Two
SUPERIORITY

You shall not make for yourself a graven image
Exodus 20:4

> Greater love has no man than this, that a man lay down his life for his friends (John 15:13). If Christ has not been raised then . . . your faith is in vain (1 Cor. 15:14).

When I stepped for the first time into Saint Peter's Cathedral in Rome, I was unprepared. Never have I been so impressed with a cathedral for its beauty, its grandeur, its significance. Neither words nor pictures can fully describe this edifice; it must be experienced.

The vast sanctuary was bathed in a warm, soft light in sharp contrast to the legion of dimly-lighted structures elsewhere. As we walked reverently through the cathedral, listening carefully to our guide, I was moved by the solemnity of the visitors. Although it was unnecessary, I wanted to whisper when I conversed. The immensity of this house of the Lord overwhelmed me. The splendid ceiling, the gold leaf, its mosaic artistry, the altar, the statuary all added to my awe. When I viewed the remains of one of the late popes, unbelievably well-preserved beneath an overlay of gold, he seemed to be alive.

I was deeply moved as I watched the crowd paying homage to a departed leader of their church. We moved along slowly with the throng toward a large statue of Saint Peter, the apostle for whom this edifice was named—a tribute rarely surpassed in the modern world. As we filed past the statue, many bowed to kiss or caress its foot. Drawing nearer, I saw that a considerable part of the foot had been worn away by the affectionate caresses of innumerable admirers.

As I looked around, many visible symbols caught my attention. There was no doubt that this was a sacred shrine. Everything pointed in that direction. The question which must be raised is this: When does an image cease being an aid to worship and become an object of worship?

I am sure that many devout believers paid homage to the image of Saint Peter with no intention of worshiping him. I am also convinced that many who paused to caress his foot were hoping something mystical would happen. Aids to worship can go beyond the role of representation. At times the line between imagery and idolatry is exceedingly fine. In order to keep as far away from idolatry as possible, some forbid any Christian representation of any kind in church and home. Crosses, a crucifix, an artist's conception of the Carpenter from Nazareth, a symbolical etching are all excluded. Some churches display no pictorial stained glass, utilize no symbolism; neither a cross nor a candle can be found. The spirit in which this is done can be meaningful; it can also be a form of idolatry, as well, in that no imagery can become a false sign of piety.

Christianity, one way or another, refuses to applaud arrogance. Humility, even when it is a put-on, seems to be virtuous. Consequently, it is understandable that we downplay our faith lest we appear to be egotistical or conceited.

This second commandment was etched into Mount Sinai stone with quite a different purpose than the first. We are all great imitators. We readily observe and consciously or unconsciously do what others are doing, for good or otherwise. The ancient Hebrews were no different. They saw what their neighbors did when they were the sons of Abraham—and they remembered. They observed the religious Egyptians in action—and never forgot. When on their trek from Egypt to the Promised Land they picked up some new religious ideas. Putting this together was rather simple. When pressed, Aaron simply said that he melted some precious metal and presto—a golden calf emerged—their new altarpiece.

Moses was furious when he saw the idolatry. What happened? The wandering tribes of Israel had made some bad assumptions. They assumed that Moses was gone forever when he disappeared on Mount Sinai, and they liked what they had seen of their neighbors' religions. Their God was invisible; a golden calf was visible. Their leader was gone; an alternative was in order. The agony of their desert wanderings was getting worse; a new religion or an addition to their own would do no harm, possibly some good. Regardless, it took only moments to fashion a new god, in spite of the fact that centuries of monotheism weighed heavily on them; God is eternal, almighty, invisible and indivisible. Any attempt on their part to make a deity would not only be wrong, it would be folly.

It would be foolish to bow down and worship a golden calf, no matter how exquisite. It would be futile to beg for mercy from a mannequin carved in marble. It would be idiotic to seek guidance in settling a dispute by bribing a "divine" serpent or trying to ascend into heaven by climbing a totem pole. This commandment is terse: don't even try.

The God of their fathers was greater than the gods of their neighbors. The rituals and ceremonies of their religion were infinitely superior to the frenzies and indecencies that surrounded them. The words of God spoken to Adam and Noah, Abraham and Isaac, Joseph and Moses are incomparable. Translated for the twentieth century, it reads something like this: DON'T TRY TO INVENT YOUR OWN RELIGION OR CREATE YOUR OWN DEITIES—THEY WILL BE NOT ONLY INADEQUATE BUT INFERIOR.

We live in an era when it's to each his or her own. We are the guardian of our own souls, the instigators of our worship. We give this perspective a variety of names but it is always some form of humanism. This second command lays down a significant principle: the faith of our fathers is incomparable. God is eternal, omnipotent and immutable (changeless), and so is the faith He has inspired. In short, Christianity, rooted and grounded on the ancient Decalogue, is not only old, it is superior. To say so is not an act of arrogance but a ritual of obedience.

The Christian is blessed with an incomparable religion. When we compare Scriptures, deities, saviors, and doctrine, the Christian religion, built upon God's moral law and His only begotten Son, is superior. When we compare what other religions have done for their masses as well as for the individual, the Christian faith is incomparable. That is why we are warned against creating a new deity or borrowing from other religions.

The ancient Hebrews were often tempted to mimic their neighbors. This included the borrowing of religious ceremonies and practices. At times they flagrantly violated their spiritual pact with Jehovah and openly worshiped false deities. Not infrequently they harbored foreign images in secret hiding places in their homes. This commandment outlawed subtle as well as blatant idolatry, its intent as well as content. God told the Israelites that image worship was wrong, that any attempt to construct an idol was futile, that the worship of living creatures was abominable.

This commandment goes even further. God claims to be a jealous God. He doesn't want any tin god made equal to Him; He doesn't want any inferior religious system to infiltrate our worship. Jealousy is a virtue. Only the distortions of jealousy are vices. For instance, if a husband is not at all jealous of his wife, he wouldn't care what she looked like, or who admired her (and how much). This could lead to little or no regard for her well-being. On the other hand, excessive jealousy could trigger suspicion, irrational behavior and hatred. God is dealing with a righteous, wholesome jealousy. He is jealous of His position amidst phony competition, but He is also jealous of the well-being of His children.

Today, as in that ancient day, just how much of an aid is needed to assist us in worshiping the true and living God is debatable. Not only were the Hebrews allowed certain symbolic and ceremonial representations, they were divinely inspired. A look at their ceremonial system, the various sacrifices and offerings, the role of the Levites and priesthood, the blueprint for the Tabernacle, the elaborate Temple, and the exacting procedures described indicate that there was a need of several aids to enhance worship.

In the New Testamental era, early Christians were instructed to observe the ritual of the Lord's Supper regularly. Baptism was instituted, and early in church life various forms of worship were incorporated—the singing of hymns, the reading and exhortation of the Scriptures, the ministering to the needs of the needy, the settling of disputes, the collection of monies and the organization of new congregations.

Furthermore, a complete understanding of the significance of the life and death of the Messiah is not understood apart from an in-depth knowledge of the Old Testament sacrificial system, ceremonies, and symbolism.

In the preceding chapter we saw that God wants to have top priority in our lives. He wants us to determine the best aspects of life and arrange them in a carefully calculated hierarchy. In this second commandment, God wants us to know how much priority He actually expects. There is no question in God's mind as He inspired this commandment—*my way, my deity, is superior.*

God is concerned lest our faith become so commonplace, so watered down, so bland that we become tolerant of every religion and every deity. Moses was not up on the mountain long before his people did what their hearts had been yearning to do. They switched religious gears.

We parents have often heard that *all roads lead to Rome;* before long, our children will question the superiority of our faith. *Is it better? Is it the best?* Or is it merely another "pebble on the beach"? God made it clear: we are not to equate Jehovah with any other god, nor are we to equate Christianity with any other religion, cult, or creed. Our faith resides in such a different category that comparison is impractical. Why? Let's look at some of the reasons.

There is no equal to the biblical Deity or His Son Jesus Christ. The God of Abraham, Isaac, Jacob, David, Daniel, and

Paul has no equal. No other savior has defeated the tomb. Jesus not only lived, He lived a perfect life. He died voluntarily, He arose supernaturally. His teachings are marvels in wisdom as well as in style. His parables are ageless, His truths eternal, His content profound yet simple. The doctrine of the Trinity is ingenious.

I once tried to discuss the Trinity with a couple of young men who had recently been spaced out on drugs. I shall never forget how they responded when I suggested that we multiply, we don't add, to compute dimensional forms. When scribbling on a napkin that $1 + 1 + 1 = 3$ but $1 \times 1 \times 1 = 1$, one of the fellows uttered just one word: "Beautiful." I shall never forget that moment. No, we cannot comprehend the Trinity, nor can we exhaust its profundity, even with a gimmicky equation.

Other religions are actually human attempts to reach or placate a deity. Christianity is God in Christ Jesus reaching down toward man to lift him up. This concept is unique, differentiating the Christian faith from all other faiths everywhere.

Occasionally we observe a religious belief or a cultic dogma similar to Christianity. This is normal. There are truths and valuable insights in every religion, sect, and ism. Truth is truth no matter where it is found. If Jesus and Confucius at times basically said the same thing, it is understandable. However, to separate the sheep from the goats, we must ask of each religion the most critical questions. The answers to these issues will give an idea how the religion or cult will hold up. Here are some of the questions we should be asking of all faiths:

Who am I? Where did I come from? Where am I going?

What is the meaning of life? Why am I here? What should I be?

Is there life after death? Is there a heaven or a hell?

What is the nature of man? Is man basically good or evil?

Is there a Supreme Being? Who or what is He? What is He like?

Is there any way I can know right from wrong? What is sin? Can I be forgiven? How?

How can I have inner peace? How can I have peace with God? Why am I unhappy?

Why is there sickness, sorrow, premature death, deformities?

When we wrestle with these and other questions, the credibility of Christianity holds.

No other religion has been so historically concerned with the past or so preoccupied with the future. Much of Scripture is prophetic in nature. In Christianity, we need not gamble with the future. We need not grope our way among the many ideologies nor flip a coin to make a moral choice. The second commandment does teach the superiority of one faith. It is not only unwise but futile to attempt to create a deity or a religious faith, or to bow down and worship an alternative. But it is also counterproductive to be arrogant about our faith.

Where, and we ask this reverently, has any other faith been so benevolent, raised the stature of childhood and womanhood to such a commendable level, or established so many orphanages, homes for the elderly, hospitals, schools, and other humanitarian depots? What other religion has fought epidemics, purified drinking water, tilled impossible soil? What other religion has sacred writings comparable to the Bible, a savior equal to Jesus, or made such an impact on art, architecture and music?

This commandment dares the Christian to compare his faith, to put it to the test. We need not be apologetic for the superiority of our faith. Christianity is good news for the family. It works!

There is another dimension to this second commandment often overlooked by the Christian. Not only is concern manifested for the priority and supremacy of God; there is an urgency which must not be overlooked. Do not bow down to these alternative gods; don't serve them!

Guardians of the souls of children are urged to teach the next generation that God is all-knowing (omniscient), that God exists everywhere (omnipresent), that God is all-powerful (omnipotent), and that God is changeless (immutable). We know that temperaments and personalities are well established early in life; we also know that a young child is receptive to spiritual nurture. If parents wait until a child is older, it may be too late to make the strongest impression. This is why God is a jealous God; He wants the best for His people, and He wants it desperately, urgently—and it must begin with each generation. When unwise parents say that they do not want to push a child against his will and they decide to wait until the child is old enough to decide for himself, they make a tragic mistake. God never intended that a child be given this burden of responsibility. A child will grow the way he is nourished, spiritually or otherwise.

This commandment deplores a casual religious training in the home, including meaningless grace said at mealtime and redundant evening prayers, subtle nonchalance or disenchantment with church, and preoccupation with secular activities compared to sacred matters. Parents who are excited by their faith, who love their Lord, who are proud of their church, and who want more than anything to see their children grow strong spiritually and sensitive morally will reap many benefits later in life.

Children do not automatically inherit a strong faith. It is true that perhaps more is caught than taught, but it still must be taught. They must be shown the way. Their questions must be dealt with at their level of understanding. Parents must go out of their way to use the common experiences of life to illustrate the way. Television is a wonderful invention and parents and children would do well to watch TV together, to discuss what they have seen, to carefully choose programs and establish standards for what is watched. One father rewards his son with TV for reading certain recommended books. Another mother limits the TV hours per week, and the family regularly reviews the TV guide as they set up priorities for their family viewing pleasure.

Spiritual nourishment takes time and effort. Furthermore, certain aids to developing a godly character are not to be underestimated. The difference between an aid to worship and an object of worship is crucial. Children rarely take God seriously unless there is a sense of urgency in their parents. Put first things first, God says, and then take those priorities and work diligently, without apology.

Let me suggest three practical matters that are important to the family. As we progress into the Decalogue, many other practical suggestions will be made. These will serve merely as a beginning.

First, *beware of the fallacy that we can begin too soon*. We can of course be unwise in our approach to young children and create an image of God which is frightening; but we can also create a concept that God is a personal God who loves little children and is unhappy when they are naughty. Sometimes we tend to underestimate the minds and feelings of our little ones, and begin too late. God must be given top priority and His superiority made clear, or the negative effects will trickle down.

When my daughter Laurie was thirteen months old, she was fascinated by TV. One day she was watching the program *Lassie*. Someone kicked the collie and sent her yelping. This act of brutality deeply affected our year-old daughter and she cried as though her little heart would break. We didn't have a dog at the time and were amazed at her comprehension and tender feelings. Ever since then I have been careful not to underestimate the capacity for even the youngest to understand. Early impressions are often indelible—for both good and ill.

It was not too long ago that special isolated nurseries for infants of unwed mothers were discontinued because of the injurious effect caused by the deprivation of human warmth and affection. Too often I'm afraid we wait too long to establish a beachhead within a child for spiritual development.

Secondly, *beware of the danger of giving up too soon*. As children get older the home gets more hectic. Meals become irregular, schedules vary, new pressures develop, resistance to certain prescriptions begins to be felt. At the same time, the children are growing in their capacity to understand; they more clearly read our attitudes and primary interests. The result is predictable: ten-year-old sons often face their pals with a five-year-old conception of God and the Christian life; teenage daughters are physically, mentally, and socially several years ahead of their spiritual development.

As children grow, so should their parents. Their questions will get tougher and perhaps even more frequent if we have kept the lines of communication open. If not, they will rarely seek out a parent for any advice on any question after a certain age, and idolatry soon sets in.

Few question the adage that "an apple doesn't fall very far from the tree." But it also seems to be true that children have a tendency to pick up the negative traits from their parents more readily than the positive. Never can we take it for granted that the child, the school, the church automatically rule out the potential of idolatry (any substitute for the true worship and allegiance to God).

Although the good Lord condemned the use of idols, there is little doubt that He encouraged certain aids to help reinforce worship and daily life. We too must not be afraid of using aids. Images which tend to become fetishes or idols are to be avoided; however, there are many ways in which the Christian family can use aids to reinforce the ideals of the home. Plaques on the walls, biblical art, various versions of the Scriptures, Christian recordings and subscriptions, good books on the shelves, family worship programs, emphasis on holy days in the home, carefully selected friends, Christian hospitality (the impressions made in my youth because of the many guests we entertained in our home are indelible). Parents can show keen interest in work done in the church school, the children's Sunday School teacher can be invited home for a meal, the family can visit religious sites, picturesque and historic churches (at home and on vacation). Even aiming for a reasonable hour of retirement on Saturday night can help create a favorable attitude towards the Lord's Day. Making Sunday something very special is extremely wise.

Some discerning mothers post Sunday School work on the refrigerator as well as daily school efforts. If this is done, naturally and deliberately, it will not be surprising that, when children become teenagers, they will not meander into idolatry.

Thirdly, *beware of the reluctance to admit having made a mistake*. We parents are novices; seldom do we get a second chance to raise a family (and if we did I'm not sure we would do much better). We often nag, coerce, threaten our children into attending Sunday School while we simply assume that they will attend public school. Why not announce, simply but firmly, that on Sundays this family goes to church, period. Nagging, bribing, or scolding is unnecessary and injurious.

How many times have we heard the statement, "My parents forced me to go to church when I was young. No child of mine will have to go to church if he doesn't want to!" Why does this so often occur with church activities but seldom with piano lessons, swimming meets, Little Leagues, or gymnastic performances?

Forcing a child is unwise. Being firm, gently insisting, no matter what the child may think, is another matter. Children want to know where their limits are; they will never find them unless the parent shows them.

I remember getting more and more angry with my daughter one day when she was extremely stubborn. At first I was rather understanding. Then I became a bit annoyed. Finally I got tough and let her know who was boss. Later that evening she cried out in pain with a horrible earache. It took quite awhile before we isolated where the pain was. Finally we got some medication and her pain subsided. She was naughty earlier in the day, not because she wanted to frustrate her dad, but because she wasn't feeling well. That evening I knelt beside her bed, wrapped my arms around her hot little body, and told her I was sorry. And I was. I was crushed. I should have known she wasn't feeling well.

I'll never forget that moment. She took her tiny little tired arms, wrapped them about my neck, and whispered, "That's okay, Daddy. I'm sorry I was naughty." No more words were spoken. An extra long hug spoke more loudly than words. We are not perfect and God help us from trying to impress our families that we are. We know that a soft answer turns away wrath; humility also does wonders. In fact, it may be our most potent weapon against idolatry, the worship of anything irrelevant or incompetent.

FOR STUDY OR DISCUSSION

1. When does an image cease being an aid to worship and become an object of worship? Give an illustration or two.

2. What did the author mean by "wholesome jealousy"? Is this important in a marriage? Between parents and children? Between a single parent and a child? How can this jealous nature turn on us?

3. How tolerant should we be of other religions, cults, or sects?

4. Explain the fallacy of the adage: "All roads lead to Rome."

5. In what ways is our faith in God and in Jesus Christ superior?

6. What are some of the truths common to most religions? Are there some valuable teachings in most religions and cults? How do you explain this? Do you know of any cult or sect which is 100 percent true? How do we measure them?

7. What are some of the most important questions we should be asking?

8. Who are the chief guardians of the souls of children?

9. What are the implications of the saying, "An apple doesn't fall very far from the tree"?

10. What are some of the aids you can use in your home to make your faith more relevant?

Chapter Three
SOLEMNITY

You shall not take the name of the Lord your God in vain
Exodus 20:7

Our Father who art in heaven, hallowed be thy name (Matt. 6:9).

As a student at the University of Minnesota, I worked at several sorority houses. In the midst of the hectic rush of the noon meal one day, the grocery boy arrived late, whistling a happy tune. Looking for a good landing strip on which to dump his groceries, he neatly stacked them on the work table where the cook had planned to lay out the noontime spread. When she discovered what this innocent redhead had done, she let him have it with a volley of profanity that would have made a vulgar lumberjack wince.

Red took a step back, placed his cap over his heart, and solemnly questioned, "Ma'am, do you eat out of that same mouth?" I shall never forget that moment.

This third declaration of the Decalogue, chiseled in stone, does deal with profanity. But it goes far beyond that.

Language is an extremely sensitive subject. It is first learned in the home, as da-da and ma-ma are quickly identified by both parent and child. It is also learned in the home that language has unusual power. "That's mine!" "Gimme" "Billy did it" and "I don't know" soon become weapons as well as expressions.

Grammar is also learned in the home—both good and poor. However, sometimes parents have flawless grammar but their children do not. Vocabularies are built early in life. When parents take the time and effort necessary to use language to its fullest, not only vocabularies but grammar will be enhanced. Sensitivities to the feelings of others develop along with language as well as discretion in the kind of language used. A child may pick up vulgarisms or profanity in school or in the neighborhood, but these will not be practiced at home without penalty, shame, or guilt, if the home is in tune with the third commandment.

For 400 years, the families of Jacob lived in Egypt. Initially, when Pharaoh knew Joseph well, the sons of Jacob probably lived in luxury. Unfortunately, their little brother, who had risen to the rank, shall we say, of prime minister, didn't live forever. Time passed and Joseph was forgotten. His family had grown into a sizeable nation within a nation, threatening the Egyptians from within.

Rather than risk an uprising, the Pharaoh forced the hapless tribes of Jacob into a more severe forced labor. Finally, the pressure was unbearable and this is where Moses entered the picture.

Well educated in the house of Pharaoh, Moses was superbly equipped to do what was necessary; he led the people out of captivity. He was an aggressive leader, a man of intense feeling, a gifted judge, highly literate and godly. As the Israelites prepared the Passover Feast and fled from the presence of the tyrannical ruler, Moses' problems were only beginning.

Crossing the Red Sea by miracle impressed the twelve tribes of Jacob momentarily. Before long their morale sagged, their self-esteem dwindled, and it was only a matter of time before there was serious trouble on the Sinai desert. The hit-and-run attacks by wandering, unfriendly nomads took their toll. Families were divided against themselves. Frustration, anger, malice, revenge, thievery, slander, infidelity and even murder swept through their ranks. Long lines waiting for the justice and judgment of Moses virtually wore him out until he reorganized the people, handling only the most serious offenses himself.

What had gone wrong? This third commandment says it all: The tribes of Israel failed to take God seriously. They ignored the wisdom and oral traditions of Abraham, Isaac, and Jacob. They forgot all about Joseph and his godly posture. They were caught between Egypt, their old stomping ground, and the land of milk and honey. Husbands mistreated wives, wives were unfaithful, children were disrespectful. Property was no longer sacred, neither was human life. A man's word no longer was trustworthy. The pomp and circumstance, the idols and rituals of Egypt dimmed the sacrifices and ceremonies made to the invisible God of Abraham.

After God had reminded the people of His priority and superiority, He then thundered something like this: YOU BETTER TAKE ME SERIOUSLY OR YOU WON'T SURVIVE. Reverence for the name of God is the starting point but it goes far beyond.

ABUSING GOD'S NAME IN LANGUAGE

There are many ways in which language can be abusive. *Profanity* is the term commonly used when defining the irreverent; it is the disregard, the defamation of anything considered reverent. Any frivolous or blasphemous degradation of that which is sacred is profane. In the broader sense, all things are classed as sacred (holy) or profane (mundane). Consequently, profanity ranges from a blatant, abusive cursing to levity where the sacred is degraded, mocked or made commonplace. Holy utterances used in an unholy manner is profanity, but profane utterances may or may not be necessarily unholy. We should not lump coarse language, vulgarity and crudity in the category of profanity although they certainly are profane.

Swearing and *cursing* are often used synonymously with profanity. Swearing, not in the positive sense of making an oath, is a negative form of dishonor, an empty, meaningless use of the name of deity to solemnize something the person never fully intended to uphold. Scripture refers to this as "vain oblations." Cursing, on the other hand, involves a deliberate intent on the part of the individual to wish misfortune, evil, or doom upon another. This is done casually by an unthinking or insensitive curse emitted habitually; or it can be the result of a deliberate attempt to damn or damage.

Lip service is also a violation of this command. Saying something but not meaning it, halfheartedness, glib promises, merely going through the motions, the failure to take God seriously are all condemned. Singing spiritual psalms and reciting *The Lord's Prayer* but not meaning any or much of it is condemned as lip service, one of the most common forms of violation of this command.

Obscenity differs from profanity in that it may or may not employ sacred expressions. Obscenity abuses the intimate and highly personal aspects of human existence and degrades them in varying ways. Crude, repulsive, loathsome, lewd descriptions of intimate personal relationships are obscene. Obscenity often attempts to cause sexual excitement or lust. Pornographic language is obscene. Obscene language is often accompanied by cursing and profanity, creating the most repulsive, degraded form of language possible.

Slang can also be profane. Slang, although widely employed and often very expressive and hardly profane, must always be considered a possible euphemism for profanity and cursing. In many instances, slang is used as a substitute for a stronger, more obviously profane expression but it is used in the same tone of voice, with an identical inflection, and often is mistaken for the original profane utterance.

The language of Christians is often punctuated with profane euphemisms. One day I tried to illustrate this in a rather profane way by fabricating a parable of a minister who attempted to dramatize this point to his congregation. As he stood before them, he said, "My dear people, I can't remember where the *heck* I put my *darn* sermon notes. *Jeez* but that makes me mad. *Gosh darn* it all." Slang may be more profane than we've been led to believe.

Levity is also a form of profanity. There is a time and a place for levity. Humor, tall tales, jokes and the like are here to stay. This is good. Life without humor would be most dreary. Some preachers, great ones at that, are memorable for their gift of humor. But levity can be abused. Levity is a lightness of behavior, a lack of proper seriousness. Although we must relax at times and hang loose, timing is important. A young minister once got into trouble when he referred to Jesus Christ and the disciples as "JC and the boys." His levity may have been better received today than when it was uttered but we must be sure to guard against making levity, a necessary ingredient in life, inappropriate.

Perjury is another way in which this command can be broken. Oaths are often solemnized by upholding the right hand, by placing a hand on the Bible, by using the name of the Almighty. Perjury is swearing to a statement known to be false or willful utterance of false evidence under oath. To testify wrongly is a violation of both the third and the ninth commandments. God's name is never to be abused.

Blasphemy reveals another overtone in using God's name in vain. This profane kind of utterance is an impious or irreverent action concerning God or sacred things. It goes further, however, in that it becomes a crime when the blasphemer assumes the rights of qualities of God. A person can blaspheme not only God and sacred things, but he can blaspheme life itself, holding nothing reverent or important.

Familiarity breeds contempt—casualness is the watchword of our society. We call our leaders Jack, Bobby, Dick, Jerry and Jimmy. Dr. Graham goes by Billy. Many pastors prefer to be called by their first names. Dr. Spock was called Ben by his sons. God is not immune to this mood; He has been called the "Man Upstairs" and other familiar expressions. The ancient Hebrews considered the name of their God to be so reverent they would not utter His name but spelled it without vowels (YHWH) so it couldn't be pronounced. This whole area needs rethinking. We must not only be concerned with the person involved but the office. God is not only the person Jesus of Nazareth; He is the Creator of the universe, its Architect, and, yes, a personal friend. A too casual approach could eventually breed contempt; a conscious, holy reverence for His name will not only give honor and dignity, it will help give the next generation a more holy legacy.

Vulgarity adds still another dimension. This is characterized by ignorance or lack of good upbringing. Crude, coarse, unrefined attitudes toward the sacred aspects of life, including the triune God, is a direct violation of this law. A vulgar attitude toward the sacred will make it commonplace or profane. Besides, this kind of attitude is so easily caught by the incoming generation.

Hypocrisy is also condemned. Jesus made this clear right after the lesson in praying when He underscored the sacredness of God's name: *hallowed be thy name*. Certain men enjoyed fasting because they could distort their faces in public to show the people how holy they were. Jesus challenged this hypocrisy by telling them to fast in private, before God only. Fasting would then lose its charm. For ages people have loved to laud the name of the deity for their own glory; others obstruct the pathway to eternal life because of a holier-than-thou conduct. Many use the name of God in vain—in other words, without benefit. Many who say "Lord, Lord" will never see the inside of the kingdom of heaven. Going through the motions is a form of profanity, a tragic occurrence in our human predicament.

God is a personal friend, not a pal. God is the highest form of nobility conceivable to mankind, but He is not unapproachable. Somewhere between a folksy, palsy approach and a trembling, awestruck attitude lies the way to enter into the presence of the living God. If it helps to use the vernacular, we should approach God in reverence this way. If we prefer to pray with the archaic *thee* and *thou*, no one should despise this route. The important thing is to hold the person and the office of the Almighty God in the highest possible esteem. Anything less than this is profane. And the best place to guarantee this is in the home.

ABUSING GOD'S NAME FOR EVIL PURPOSES

God's name is also abused for evil purposes. Many have felt that the holy, eternal deity could be coerced by calling His name. Even Satanists use the name of the holy one of Israel in dealing with the devil. Men in trouble have literally begged, if not ordered, the Almighty to bail them out. If He did, they promptly forgot Him; if not, they cursed Him. How could He win? Magicians, sorcerers and witches have long evoked the name of God for their incantations. Children have been sacrificed to weird deities by priests feverishly chanting magical names of God, often long chains of names. The third utterance of the "thunderstones" warns us not to use the name of God for evil purposes.

A young lady came to my office and before long we were discussing the subject of evil forces and parlor games. Some of her friends had become more than enchanted with an Ouija board. Not only were they amused, they were fascinated. After several sessions, the Ouija board told the girls to go to a certain address at a specified time. Then they began to feel an eerie, uncanny spirit about the whole thing. Luckily, they quit while still ahead.

Spiritualism, seances, mediums, occultism (belief in the existence of supernatural agencies that can be known and communicated with), astrology, fortune-telling, clairvoyance, visions, trances and black magic are all involved in this commandment.

With the multitude of cults and isms flourishing, with national figures attempting to communicate with the dead, with fortune-tellers making astounding predictions, with a wholesale belief in astrology, discerning parents must concern themselves. Just as there is considerable difference between prayer and black magic, there is a considerable difference between worshiping God and playing with the occult.

God's name is not magic, black, white or otherwise. His name, however, lends considerable support to many individuals in a variety of ways. A bizarre way of using God's name for an evil purpose is illustrated by the maverick who began to court one of the finest young Christian ladies in town. In order to impress her, the clever suitor sized up her greatest strengths. Since she was a very devout Christian, he mastered the Christian vocabulary. Before long he could strut like a saint of long standing. He could pray like a deacon. Impressing everyone, he erased his maverick reputation and established himself as a noble young Christian. When this charming lady became his bride, he promptly discarded his facade and returned to his old rotten self.

Con artists of every imaginable description have hidden beneath the cloak of respectability, using the name of the deity in bilking innocents. Hypocrites abound everywhere. In fact, you do not find counterfeits of anything that has no value. This is quite a tribute to the Christian faith.

Our children should be warned about imposters; they should be told that hypocrites do abound; they should know that people are imperfect, that the true test of faith is not found in people but in Christ Jesus; and they should be told that the highest authority is God's Word, not ours. Youth so grounded do not crumble when they discover that their heroes are fallible.

BLESSINGS TO THOSE WHO HONOR GOD'S NAME

This stanza of the Decalogue has a chorus written in a major key. So far we have discussed some of the dangers in misappropriating the name of God. There is also a great blessing in store for those who use His name aright.

When I began my pastoral ministry, I served a small pioneer church in the heart of cherry country near Traverse City, Michigan. In joining the local ministerium, I quickly learned that the association had certain traditional responsibilities. Among these was a ritual called "The Blessing of the Blossoms." Every spring the ministers were responsible for a religious ceremony which involved leading a procession through a cherry orchard when the blossoms were at their peak. The ritual also included a ministerial invocation upon the orchards, asking God's blessings on the blossoms.

My first impression was to chalk this off as a semi-pagan custom—a kind of ecclesiastical white magic. The more I thought about it the more I began to realize that although this could be a form of celestial coercion it could also be a spiritual reminder that without the eternal Creator of the universe in control of nature, nothing, not even cherries, could exist. The cherry growers, whether they realized it or not, were at the mercy of the elements. The precarious balance would depend upon the minister who could either chant a kind of contemporary white magic as he invoked God's blessing, or he could humbly beseech the Lord's mercy and remind the people of their spiritual heritage and consequent responsibilities. The invocation of righteously calling upon the name of the Lord at the outset of every significant as well as trivial act is not out of order.

Prayer can be a blessed experience; it can also be vain babbling. When we pray we communicate with God; we do not coerce Him. We pray in thanksgiving; we pray in despair; we pray when we need or want something; we pray simply when we hunger for fellowship with our Redeemer. We pray in private and we pray in public—we pray alone and we pray in unison. Prayer is a wonderful experience of taking the name of God seriously.

The thief on the cross prayed and found himself in paradise with the Man who hung on the center cross. He preferred to be with Jesus rather than spend eternity with his old buddy; he wanted to be saved from his sins more than he wanted to be saved from the cross. He couldn't kneel, nor could he fold his hands—he probably didn't even close his eyes as he looked at his newly discovered Friend and Saviour. But he prayed. It was in public, it was audible, it was brief but to the point, it was answered. Prayer is a wonderful way of using God's name; in fact, it is difficult to pray and curse at the same time. If we would teach our children to pray, they would find it unnecessary and extremely distasteful to be profane.

When God's name is used in our judicial system to solemnize oaths, it is natural. To be guilty of perjury is a violation not only against man but against a holy, just Supreme Being. God's name is a mighty name. We can keep it that way by recognizing His *priority*, acknowledging His *superiority*, and by taking Him *seriously*.

J.B. Phillips has done us a favor in penning the book *Your God Is Too Small*. The wise parent guides his or her child into an awesome reverence of the Almighty, giving him a high regard for the name above all names. At times our concept of God gets out of proportion—it gets too small.

One of life's tragedies is to see a father who has matured in matters of secular importance but leads his family spiritually with the same concept of God he had when he was a lad of ten. We realize that God changes not, but our concept of Him does, and it should be growing steadily through prayer, commitment, study and worship. If Dad's God is too small, it is quite likely that *Johnny's* God will not be adequate either. Taking God seriously is a lifelong business.

Following are practical suggestions for taking God and our faith seriously:

Language—One of the greatest teachers in the home is language. Most Christian homes are not profane. Cursing is rare. However, the home is often the place where the guard is down. Husbands and fathers sometimes talk at home to their wives and children as they would never do in public. A woman might nag at home but never anywhere else. Words can hurt, and language at home is often laced with barbs. Tempers flare. Incredible? Hardly. Home is often the roughest place on earth as it prepares children for the tough arena of life ahead.

At home we often vent our frustrations on innocent members of the family. A bad day in the office can result in a horrible dinner hour at home. Home is where we make petty comments about people. Consequently, we often must mind our tongues more at home than anywhere else! We must watch our slang, our gossip, our conversation, our Freudian slips, digs and innuendos. There are tiny (and not so tiny) ears that don't miss a thing. God's reputation—and ours—is at stake.

Prayer—We can make prayer in the home a beautiful occasion or we can make it nothing but a dreary routine. Grace and devotions at mealtime can be a hallowed moment or a meaningless ritual. Bedtime prayers can be merely habit-forming (not altogether a bad thing, incidentally). How often do we sit down on the edge of the bed and discuss the ups and downs of the day before prayer, using these precious moments to build up our child in the nurture of the Lord? There are excellent books on prayer, and many fine children's prayers that could be read and discussed. Even a hymn could be read as an aid to prayer, and suggestions of people and subjects needing our prayer support are highly in order. This will involve some effort on our part, but it will pay rich dividends. The disciples asked the Lord to teach them to pray; our children are asking us to do the same.

Laughter—Too many of our homes have lost the ring of laughter. We often take ourselves too seriously. Serving Christ is a joyous adventure, and we ought to make our homes echo with laughter and mirth. Although frivolity can be a bad thing, this is not what we are suggesting; our Christian homes are often too somber. Why? Perhaps it is due to the fact that we realize the consequences of a life without Christ, without values, without goals and ideals; so we try *too* hard. We know the stakes are high, and to keep our children from "getting burned" we pour the hose on them too often. Somewhere between making life a joke and making it a somber institution, we must strive toward a meaningful atmosphere where our children will want to live and where they will find nourishment for their souls. We *can* be too solemn as we take our "religion" too seriously.

Perjury—This is one of the quickest roads to parental suicide known. Making promises to children and failing to keep them has destroyed the credibility of many parents. No wonder the youthful slogan stuck: "Never trust anyone over thirty." Although a distortion, there is more than a shade of truth here.

Idle threats fall into the same category. A threat to spank that is never fulfilled may be more dangerous than an actual spanking. The fact is that Johnny doesn't really want to get away with murder. Families are notorious in committing unintentional "perjury."

Hypocrisy—We are all hypocrites at times, unless we are perfect. The kind of hypocrisy which is dangerous is not an occasional slip, but the deliberate, sanctimonious masquerade. A child soon knows where his father stands. A man with no guile will deeply impress his son. The parent who preaches equal rights in the church business session but belittles minority groups at home is liable to send a son or daughter into a spiritual dead end. The parent who wrongly treats his family to dinner on a company expense account is doing the same. Grace said before a meal like this would probably be better left unsaid. If we take God seriously we must avoid every form of hypocrisy.

Lip service—The family falls into this trap in two ways: the first is to merely go through the motions of a spiritual life in which the vitality and urgency are missing. The other way is to fail to listen. We parents can turn off our kids in a hurry. We are tired, we are busy, we don't want to be bothered, and so we nod assent but "haven't heard a word." Our children's words go in one ear and out the other. It takes *time* to listen; it takes *desire* to listen; it takes *effort* to listen. It may involve us in a problem bigger than we want. After awhile, the child catches on, realizes he's a pest, and the damage is done. Communication begins at the cradle where we coo back to the infant who has our heart all wrapped up in its tiny little fists; it continues through the baby-talk stage and keeps right on. Someone wisely said that it's not so much the *quantity* of time we give our children as it is the *quality*. Parents are busy people, but we better not be too busy! Children need both quality and quantity of listening.

Urgency—In many Christian families there is not much of a sense of urgency when it comes to spiritual matters. Worship is important not because of its eternal purpose but because it's the expected thing to do; lying becomes uncouth, not a sin; stealing is considered unfair, not a violation of God's word; sin is only immaturity. Nothing in this kind of home could be interpreted as really profane, but nothing is sacred either. Bland environments create bland people. It's often assumed that the tranquility and solidarity of a home is due to the adequacy of the members of the family, not because the household is committed to the Lord. Therefore, a secular mentality overrides the spiritual. When all goes well, God seems quite unnecessary; when the going gets difficult, God may be blamed. On the other hand, parents excited about their faith usually transfer this excitement to the rest of the family.

This commandment reminds us to keep God first in our homes. God's name is holy; His title is reverent; His office is strategic. God wants us to remember that His name is solemn and that building a Christian home is a sacred trust. If we put God first, consider Christianity the greatest faith on earth, and take what God says seriously with a sense of urgency, our homes will be built on a solid foundation.

FOR STUDY OR DISCUSSION

1. How important are the early years in life for determining the direction a child's language will take (vocabulary, grammar, inflection, accent, purity, sensitivity)?
2. Is it easy to tame the tongue? If not, why not?
3. Language is one of the differentiating characteristics separating humans from non-humans. How would you explain this?
4. What is wrong with taking God's name in vain? What is wrong with using euphemisms (gol, gosh, jeez)?
5. Should a Christian pay special attention to his or her language (grammar, vocabulary, cursing, vulgarity, slang, blasphemy, etc.)? Why?
6. What does "lip service" have to do with this commandment?
7. What is "black magic"? What is "white magic"? How does this commandment address this subject?
8. Put the third commandment into a positive statement. You shall . . .

What are some of the opposites to *lightly, irreverently, nonchalantly, mechanically, haphazardly, casually, insincerely*, etc.?

9. How can we take ourselves too seriously, too somberly?
10. How can we take God "seriously with a sense of urgency"?

Chapter Four
FRAILTY

Remember the sabbath day to keep it holy
Exodus 20:8

Come to me, all who labor
and are heavy laden, and I
will give you rest (Matt.
11:28).

For many children, Sundays are about as welcome as a cobra in a cradle.

The Sabbath has an inglorious history. We have long squabbled about the Sabbath versus Sunday. We have turned it into a holiday instead of a holy day. It has been ingloriously exploited and blue laws have been passed to force petty prohibitions on the Sabbath. The Puritans did their best to legislate piety, especially through a strict adherence to Sabbath laws. Evidently the only way to worship God was to make sure that no one enjoyed Sunday. The Pilgrims punished people for not going to church on Sundays, and punished them if they went anywhere else. Before long many of the laws of the church became the law of the land, and then the pendulum reversed its swing.

We have seen tragic results because of attempts to legislate piety. By forcing people to attend church, parents and ministers alike have made the same mistake. Youth often rebel when forced to attend church, and throw away many spiritual values in the process. Sanctimonious church-goers drive unbelievers away in droves. Hypocrites exist everywhere but seem to be more visible in the church.

Years ago, church membership was low and attendance, proportionately, was high. Today the reverse is true. An astoundingly low percentage of church members attend regularly. Church attendance among American youth drops off sharply as they approach twenty-five years of age. College seniors attend far less than freshmen, but this may be changing.

Among those who still attend church with some degree of regularity, many have rather vague reasons for their attendance. Youth, including children, are asking some provocative questions. They want to know why attending church is important. They want to know why Sunday should be different. They want to know why it's alright to go to the beach on some weekends (but not every weekend). They also want to know why some stores thrive on Sundays, why Sunday sports are so big, why so many churches are jammed only at Christmas and Easter, etc.

With these questions demanding answers, we will explore five aspects of this subject that seek a deeper understanding. Unless Christian parents are able to grapple adequately with this, they probably will be unable to convince the next generation of the importance of the Sabbath.

THE BIBLICAL SABBATH

One of the most burning problems in the Sinai desert was monotony. Mile after mile of weariness and sand without the amenities of forests and lakes, fields of clover and grazing cattle, takes its toll.

As the Israelites trudged through the desert, avoiding the caravan routes, villages, and settlements while searching for water and safe passage, boredom was inevitable. Every day seemed the same. Often I have sensed this phenomenon while making hospital rounds—many patients lose all sense of time—every day is alike.

Since the wandering tribes had never been where they were going they didn't know precisely what lay ahead. The 400-year-old visions of the Promised Land began to fade. So did the frustrations and harassment caused by the tyrannical Egyptian taskmasters. They wanted to turn around and go back. They complained about the food and the water and the routing chosen by Moses; they wearied of breaking camp and answering questions: "Daddy, are we there yet?"

These people needed something to look forward to. When they looked for the Promised Land they saw a mirage, if they saw anything. But God knew better. He knew they needed more than a dream, more than "pie in the sky." They needed a regular rhythm to their life. While tromping on the desert sands, one day wore into the next until there was no difference between Tuesday and Wednesday, Saturday and Sunday. The Sabbath presumably had disappeared.

Remembering the Sabbath "to keep it holy" meant two things. First, the twelve tribes would be guaranteed one day a week that would be totally different from the others. It would in effect be an oasis in their desert. There would be no tromping on the hot sands, no packing and unpacking of tents, no slaughtering of lambs or cooking, no repair of frazzled goatskins. It would be a day of rest, a change of pace, a day to be eagerly awaited.

But it would be more than that. Second, it would be a festive day, a day when they would worship, not only as individuals but as a people. If the Sabbath were kept alive, their rituals and ceremonies would come alive. The kids would get excited. Father would be the household priest and the official priests would make sacrifices. Horns would blow, and where the Sabbath was kept the other religious festivals would come alive. A deeper awareness of the Almighty would transform their mundane existence into one of meaning. Evidently God knew His creation. If the Sabbath were observed, there was hope for the nation. Perhaps this is why this is one of the positive commands: REMEMBER . . . TO KEEP IT HOLY because it in turn will keep you holy.

The biblical Sabbath was the seventh day of the week, beginning at sundown and continuing for twenty-four hours. The transition from the Sabbath to Sunday is a stumbling stone for many. The seventh-day Sabbath is mentioned many times in the New Testament. This is not disputed; nor does Scripture suggest that the Sabbath should be changed from its current form to Sunday. Therefore, to argue that Sunday should rightfully be the Lord's Day, and the Sabbath is no longer valid, more is needed than words of Scripture or the passage of time. Rather than debate the issue fully, let's look at a simple, brief story of the transition from the ancient Sabbath to the Christian Sunday.

In the creation, God rested on the seventh day. In this way He blessed the Sabbath and hallowed it. The Hebrews were given explicit instructions for the observance of this day. Jesus taught in the synagogue on the Sabbath. He also severely rebuked those who missed the spirit of the Sabbath.

Because of the hardness of the hearts of the people, the Sabbath was forced to take upon itself some cumbersome observances lest its intent be forgotten. Therefore, pious Jews took meticulous precautions to see that the Sabbath was upheld. Jesus broke through many of these impositions by healing on the Sabbath as well as defending His disciples when they winnowed grain in their hands to ward off their Sabbath-day hunger.

When the resurrection of the Messiah occurred, the first day of the week became very meaningful to the disciples. As time progressed, Sunday, the first day of the week, became increasingly more sentimental and conducive to worship as it helped distinguish the Christian community from its Jewish counterpart.

During the second century after Christ, the church fathers proclaimed Sunday a special day, not in adoration of the sun but to give instruction in holy writings, in the distribution of bread and wine, and to collect alms. Gradually, the first day of the week became the day when Christians assembled together to worship and to celebrate the Lord's Supper. As the ancient Hebrew calendar was overshadowed by Roman calculations, the Christians adopted this way of reckoning time. Although there is no question but that the world about the believers influenced their lives, there is no reason to believe that the Christians had accepted the pagan celebration of the day of the sun (Sun day) with all its implications as their holy day.

Gradually, certain attributes of the ancient Sabbath were transferred to Sunday. Not only was this a day of worship but a day of rest. To this day there is a close association between the Sabbath and the Christian Lord's Day. Sunday, for Christians, has become God's holy day, a fulfillment of the Sabbath, not an abolishment of it.

The Lord's Day gradually became universalized. It was a good thing for the church to have a uniform day in which all of its members could come together for fellowship, prayer, reading of the Scriptures, singing of hymns, preaching and the sacraments. Eventually Sunday was beneficial to the entire civilized society. As abuses developed, both church and state attempted to safeguard its blessings and minimize grievances by legalizing the Lord's Day. It is not uncommon for Sunday observances to be right in the center of community controversies. The wise recognize the value in keeping Sunday separate from other days. They also know that opportunities can and do negate the spirit of the Lord's Day. This brings us to the second consideration.

HUMANITY IS FRAIL

At times we find it difficult to admit that we are human, not superhuman. We are able to solve baffling perplexities in natural science only to become unable to cope with certain social situations. A tycoon can run an empire from his skyscraper suite but can be helpless in managing his teenage son. We are fragile, we do make mistakes, we cannot solve some of our problems; in other words, this commandment reminds us that we are human.

Although Sunday comes at the outset of the week, it does something quite significant: it separates a period of six days from another period of six days. It interrupts, it breaks up the routine, it gives life a rhythm. In other words, if we would work, work, work, seven days a week, fifty-two weeks a year, something most unfortunate would occur. We would crack up—physically, mentally, emotionally, spiritually. We are not supermen; we are not angels either. We are strictly human, and God knows this because He designed us. Therefore, God instructed us to break up the monotony and rigors of life by knocking off one day a week. We can function for a while on a seven-day week, but not for long; individuals and civilizations alike must live with this universal principle. Otherwise, minds begin to strain; emotions are troubled; nerves are stretched too far; muscles tense. Before long, days become too long, efficiency decreases, boredom sets in, the mind gets stale. God ordained the concept of the Sabbath and the early church was wise in transferring these concepts to the Lord's Day.

LEISURE CAN BE LETHAL

Six days you shall labor. With a seven-day week, God intended that we occupy ourselves for six days. There is an infinite amount of wisdom in this commandment. Not only are we to routinely observe the one day, we are to keep busy the rest of the time. Franz Alexander highlights this in a chapter in his book, *The Western Mind in Transition*: "Retirement Neurosis and Malignant Boredom." Remembering the adage that "idleness breeds mischief," too much leisure creates problems similar to that of overwork.

With prospects for shorter and shorter working weeks, we ought to be concerned with the creation of excessive spare time. Some of this can be absorbed through planned recreation, hobbies, do-it-yourself projects, travel, and moonlighting. It is true that the creative, energetic person could probably occupy all the leisure time he could get, but there are many who will not know what to do; some will dissipate these hours of leisure; others will be overly bored.

To argue that this commandment is expecting each Christian without exception to work six days a week at some gainful employment may be missing the spirit of what God has in mind. One professional with enormous resources may devote one day a week to his or her profession in order to give the rest of the time to philanthropic work. Another individual may work six long, hard days and then plow fifty percent or perhaps even more of his earnings into Christian endeavors. The idea is not necessarily eight hours a day for six days a week, but keeping the cancer of excessive leisure from striking.

This commandment is trying to tell us that we need a change of pace, a day of relaxation, and certainly regular moments of worship and instruction. However, there seems to be another dimension to this principle. When we refuse to work, we place an unnecessary burden upon our family and/or community. Welfare lines bulge with those who can work but will not. Not only does this create an economic burden on a society, it reduces a person's self-esteem. The sense of pride, the good feeling of fatigue after an honest day's work, the nobility of accomplishment become impossible.

Once I bailed a nineteen-year-old out of jail. He seemed to be most grateful and promised faithfully to repay me within two weeks. As far as I knew, he did not work a single day after he was set free, nor did he try. The real tragedy was not economic but what happened to him as a man. He avoided me, not because he owed me something but because he owed himself something. Because he refused to work he lost his self-esteem, his belief in himself, his reason for existence.

Many of us are inclined to be undisciplined, even the youngest. Years ago I overheard my wife saying to our four-year-old, "Scottie, I have a little job for you to do tomorrow." Cruel? No, not at all. It wasn't a bit too early to allow Scott to become a participating, responsible member of the Seagren household. Years from now he'll thank us for this; so will society.

After some nine years of college teaching, I rarely found assignments handed in early. Libraries were also victimized by the last minute rush as term papers became due. Many students took life casually and then crammed desperately before an exam. Many of us are a wee bit lazy, and find self-discipline difficult. Medical personnel testify to the difficulty patients have in dieting, exercising, following orders. When a person develops a bad habit of wasting time or lacks self-discipline, this command literally speaks with clarity: leisure can be lethal as well as beneficial.

CORPORATE WORSHIP IS NECESSARY

A few individuals prefer to do things alone, but the majority of us prefer the company of others. In fact, we crave fellowship and companionship. We are so constituted. A melancholic introvert may prefer to isolate himself somewhere, and he may be a very productive person intellectually, but he is still an exception. We love to be with others, especially those we enjoy.

Scripture abounds with admonitions for the individual to commune regularly with God. The psalmists reflect this in both adoration and agony. They wept for their sins and they shouted for joy in the presence of Jehovah. They were exhorted to meditate in the law day and night, casually and systematically, no doubt. Daniel prayed three times a day. Jesus prayed so earnestly and probably so long that His disciples fell asleep. Numerous examples can be given about the necessity of a personal, private communion with the Almighty.

At the same time, Scripture insists that we come together to worship—to sing hymns and spiritual psalms, to break bread, to receive tithes and offerings, to hear the holy writings expounded. In the Old Testament, the Sabbath was created to give a day of rest and relaxation from pressing duties, to give an opportunity to regroup faculties, but it also was given for worship. Resting on the Sabbath was not enough; a change of pace, necessary and beneficial, was not enough. Each person, as one member of the human race, needed to come together with another to worship the true and the living God.

Worship is at least twofold: (1) it tells our God and Saviour that we are grateful for our salvation; (2) it also nourishes us spiritually, making us blessed of God. Going to church does not make us holy; nor do only holy people go to church. Many attend because their souls are empty, their lives hollow, their habits disabling. Many attend because it's the thing to do, it's expected of them. Some attend to hear great oratory, listen to a fine choir or become engulfed in a solemn ritual. There is no single reason why people go to church.

Some disregard the church except at times of baptism, catechism, marriage, death, and holy days. Others go regularly, rain or shine. Some attend one hour a week on Sunday mornings; others go twice (or more) on the Lord's Day and often during the week. Some services are exceedingly simple, devoid of all ritual; others are highly liturgical. In some congregations the family is scattered in every direction (extended sessions, children's church, nurseries; preference for peers); other churches have retained the "family pew" and the whole family worships together (which seems to be a great idea).

Each family, each individual must work out its own program according to individual needs and situations. However, this commandment insists on something the family must not overlook: corporate (united, combined) worship is not an option. We are admonished to worship regularly at least once a week. There is no fixed hour; no set amount of the day is designated for worship. For some it may be an hour; for others it may be longer. The most important thing is to keep at it, regularly, not allowing trivial or even important matters keep us away from worshiping with other believers on the Lord's Day. Worshiping via radio and television, possibly acceptable now and then (and sometimes necessary), robs us of this communion with others.

Worship on the Lord's Day should not be substituted for a personal, daily communion with the Lord God. God never intended that the spiritual nourishment of His people be limited to one hour a week. The facts speak for themselves: the soul that worships, communes with its Creator, and prays only one hour a week probably finds itself starved spiritually although maybe not realizing it.

We also make the mistake of not attending church because we "don't get anything out of it." The preacher may be as dry as chalk, the choir may sound like a rusty hinge, the organ may have a good case of asthma, and there may be a sanctimonious hypocrite in every pew. This is beside the point, really. We do not attend church only to receive; we come to give. We lift up our hearts in adoration to our God; we sing psalms and spiritual hymns not to make an impression but to receive a blessing; we give in the offering not because the church extols this virtue but because the salvation we have is worthy of sharing.

There is something majestic about the sound of a chorus of saints chanting in unison. There is security in knowing that we are not alone, either in our sins or in forgiveness. The genuine believer can miss a service now and then, but actually he doesn't want to, and he will make a tremendous effort to enter the sanctuary of the Lord. It is true that on some days the hearer is a bit less alert than he might be; on some days the sermon fails to come alive; the choir may even have bad days. Yet, one Sunday the believer may get a blessing from the choir or the pastoral prayer but not the sermon. Even so, there is danger in attempting to justify attendance on the basis of being specifically blessed. It is the cumulative effect that does the spiritual work—Sunday after Sunday, year after year, message upon message, anthems, Scripture, prayers, sacraments, rituals, and opportunities for fellowship. This is where the important work is done. When the believer leaves the house of God he walks a little taller and possibly a little straighter. When the unbeliever departs, he may or may not realize that he has been in the presence of One who loves him and died for him. Sooner or later the message may get through.

When parents don't care to fellowship with other believers, and merely look for faults or esoteric blessings, there is little or nothing they can do to make the Lord's Day a happy day for their children. This malady of antagonism toward the house of the Lord is contagious, most readily caught by the children of the household.

THE LORD'S DAY IS HOLY

This last dimension of the fourth commandment is important but badly misunderstood. We do need rest and relaxation, and a change of pace. Sundays are to be different from weekdays. But the eternal question is *how different*? Christians interpret Sundays in a great variety of ways. Some believe that a worship hour early Sunday morning establishes the mood for the coming week, fulfills the obligation of the day. Other congregations insist on a full day of worship including Sunday School and youth services, committee meetings, concerts, and other forms of expression. Still others center the entire worship experience around the Lord's Supper. With awesome differences within church groups as well as within individuals, no single pattern fits all situations.

This command was never intended to restrict the Christian to a day of petty decrees or to allow a wide open kind of holiday. It simply but emphatically tells us to *remember* the Lord's Day (Sabbath) to keep it holy. A colleague of mine boasted of a rather poor memory. When he forgot something, he sympathetically blamed it on his "forgetter." Many of us have forgetters that work overtime. We are told to remember (not forget) the Sabbath. In our condition of human and spiritual *frailty*, we need to be reminded, regularly, that we are human; we would allow our worship experience to lapse unless we observed it regularly and systematically. Our forgetters are ever present.

The entire day is holy, not merely the hours of regularly scheduled worship, or the irregularly scheduled times. This is where much difficulty arises.

Sundays for many children are wretched days. Perhaps this is because we try too hard to make it a meaningful, sacred time. We tend to stress the negative as the Puritans did or we go the other direction and make Sundays inconsequential. We can break the Sabbath by being too brittle, or we can be too pliable; somewhere between these extremities lies a better way. Let me suggest a few thoughts for your consideration which may help you in determining how you and your family could observe this holy day:

1. Stress the fact that God created the Sabbath for our benefit—accentuate the positive.
2. Establish a high priority for attending a worship service every Lord's Day if at all possible (vacations, long weekends,

weather, late hours on Saturday nights, illness all tend to rob us of this day with our families in God's house).

3. Plan for Sunday early in the week—look forward to it with anticipation with your family. Make Sunday a high, not a low, of the week.

4. Plan special things for Sunday, before or after worship and other responsibilities, which will make it a day of delight. Use this day to get closer to your kids. Let them help in making plans for spending the afternoon, going to see friends or relatives, etc.

5. Keep the whole day holy. This means that every aspect of the day should have a spiritual significance, not just a fraction of it. For instance, a trip to the zoo on a Sunday afternoon could be used to bring the family close together and to give the Creator credit for His great creation. Both of these could be sacred experiences. Going to the zoo could also be merely an afternoon excursion with no spiritual meaning at all.

6. Remember that the church cannot and should not try to compete with the many entertaining and exciting events that occur on the Lord's Day. Remember when the TV special *Heidi* was put on the air before a professional football game had ended? It turned out that the game finished with a dramatic upset and millions of fans were deprived of seeing this for themselves. The church is not entertainment, but sometimes we make the mistake of not realizing the difference between worship and fun. We probably can never upstage the competition of Sunday, but Sundays can still be very memorable in spite of it. Don't underestimate God's presence.

7. There are no set rules for observing the Lord's Day. When a Christian family takes the Lord's Day seriously, it realizes that all things are lawful but not all things are expedient. Some perfectly good things may be left out of the schedule not because they are wrong but because they may tend to profane the sanctity of the day.

8. Assume that children will attend church; from the time they are very young, they should simply but firmly be informed that "on Sundays this family goes to church." Period.

We do this with public school and piano lessons. Why not with church? It is too easy to allow children the unfortunate luxury of making the decision on Sunday.

9. Church attendance is not a goal, nor is keeping the Sabbath holy. These are means unto an end, not an end in itself. Many parents are stunned when youth suddenly forsake spiritual things, including the church. They think that because their offspring were uncomplaining church attenders everything was in fine order, spiritually. Churchmanship must go deeper than merely attending the public services of the congregation.

10. Don't underestimate the power of good habits. When children are schooled in the meaning of the Lord's Day and are taught to worship regularly, a worthwhile habit is being formed. Many youth favor the Lord's house and the Sabbath but have cultivated such haphazard attendance patterns in their youth that this becomes a lifelong habit. We do our children a great favor by making their worship experience meaningful and systematic.

Because we are *frail*, spiritually, mentally and physically, the good Lord created a special day for our benefit. This is why He has told us to guard it well. The Sabbath was made for us because we need it.

FOR STUDY OR DISCUSSION

1. What was Sunday like when you were a child? What is it like today? What, if any, are the significant differences?
2. How can we make Sundays more meaningful? More holy?
3. When Sunday shopping, sports, TV and weekend journeys are so important to our society, what affect does this have on the Christian family? On society at large?
4. What principles of the Old Testament Sabbath carry over into the New Testament concept of Sunday? Why do you worship on Sunday rather than Saturday? (Or why do you worship on Saturday rather than Sunday?)
5. What is good about a Thursday evening worship service

for those who cannot or prefer not to worship on Sunday? What is not good about it?

6. What is the significance of the word *Frailty* in the title of this chapter? Can you think of a better word or title?

7. What would happen to a society which exists without a Sunday-type of day each week? What happened when the USA war factories treated every day alike during World War II? Could you enjoy living without a weekend?

8. What value is there to regular worship versus spasmodic?

9. If overwork is bad, is underwork just as detrimental? How?

10. Compare corporate worship to individual worship. Do we need one or the other or both? Unless one is seriously handicapped, can we worship adequately via radio or TV? How?

Chapter Five

SECURITY

Honor your father and your mother
Exodus 20:12

And now a word to you parents. Don't keep on scolding and nagging your children, making them angry and resentful. Rather, bring them up with the loving discipline the Lord himself approves, with suggestions and godly advice (Eph. 6:4, *TLB*).

A whole generation has more or less been weaned on a philosophy which tends to encourage self-expression at the expense of inner discipline. Few would disagree that we need a healthy combination of self-expression and inner discipline, but when one is accomplished at the expense of the other, the result is unfortunate. Perhaps the pendulum has swung as far as it is going to go. If so, the question remains: How far, and how quickly, will it swing back?

Contemporary scholarship in this area is voluminous. It is difficult, if not impossible, to find an unwavering consensus in the relationship between parent and child. What is valid today may be invalid tomorrow. What now seems wise may ultimately be foolish. In the midst of this confusion, does the family turn to its own ingenuity and just plain common sense in raising a family, or can it find principles guaranteed not to corrupt the next generation? Our contention is that the Ten Commandments provide these enduring principles.

The ancient Hebrews left Egypt in a hurry. No doubt they were also in a hurry to get to the Promised Land. When the journey took much longer than they had anticipated (they actually took a much longer though safer route), the people began to have second thoughts. Doubts crept in, pushing optimism and hope out. Whenever this happens it is rarely superimposed from outside; it stems from within.

Husbands and wives began to question the wisdom and skill of Moses. They remembered the altercation he had with the Egyptian slave driver. They knew about his forty-year exile in the wilderness. They never forgot or forgave his luxurious upbringing in the courts of Pharaoh and they almost blotted out the memory of the awesome plagues and the incredible crossing of the Red Sea. Over their desert tea, supposedly when the children were asleep, they shared their misgivings. Dad checked the stars and realized they were heading south rather than east. Mom complained about the awful taste of the water. Moses received no kind words for his efforts and God took a share of the blame, too.

Meanwhile, the little ones were listening. Soon they too were complaining. Family morale began to slip and it spread from one tent to the next. As the going became more tedious, tensions rose. Respect for mother and father slipped a notch, and then another until parents were struggling with a new symptom: disrespect which eventually degenerated into incorrigibility.

When there is low morale at home, accompanied by bad blood, the atmosphere necessary to maintain decorum and instill confidence and hope is stifled. The dignity and honor of the family was threatening the very existence of the twelve tribes causing God to speak forcibly to the issue: IF YOU WANT TO SURVIVE, HONOR YOUR MOTHER AND YOUR FATHER.

THE PARENTS' ROLE

To begin, we must take a good look at the wording of this fifth command. We know the New Testament advocates that parents do nothing to provoke their children to wrath while urging them to follow the pathway walked by their parents.

Children are told to obey their parents, to observe the chain of command, etc. It is not difficult to build a strong case for the necessity of children obeying and respecting Christian parents. At the same time it would be difficult to defend an ideology which advocates that a child give blind obedience to unworthy parents, to steal when a parent says steal, to cheat, curse, or abuse their bodies. Whatever this command urges, it does not demand an unholy allegiance to nor the admiration of an unworthy parent.

The key to the commandment is found in the word *honor*. The word honor has a regality to it, a concept not very well understood by those not acquainted with royalty. Perhaps the closest we come in the United States is in addressing a judge as "Honorable Judge." Actually, the judge may be a poor neighbor or a mediocre attorney, but he or she is recognized and honored for the position he/she holds.

In other societies, an officer of the highest rank as well as the lowliest soldier would respectfully address their king "Your Honor." In a sense there are no degrees of honor: it is always the highest order. Implied within the expression is not the person but the position; the same is true of parenthood. Whether parents ever earn this honor is debatable. Probably not. That is why honor is demanded: parenting is an extremely important and difficult position. Because parenthood is so honorable its role must be respected and maintained.

THE KEY TO LONGEVITY

If parenthood plays such a strategic role there must be a reason why. This is implied in the commandment itself: *That your days may be long in the land which the Lord your God shall give you.* In other words, parenthood is the key to not only longevity, but survival. If we could survive on bread alone (or even manna which these people ate in the wilderness) spiritual dimensions to life would be unnecessary. God could have sustained His people indefinitely on the bread (manna) which *fell* out of heaven, but He didn't. Mankind could try to sustain itself forever on bread (adequate food) if that is all there is to life.

This command is talking about a principle larger than life. In other words, we are dealing with human longevity. The implication is obvious: If the ancient Hebrew people were to survive, parenthood had to be kept honorable. If people today are to survive, the family has to be kept intact. Because the heart and soul of humanity lies within the family unit, there is no viable alternative. If the reason for existence, the ethics and morals of humanity are to be carried out, it must be nurtured. This is best done generation after generation within the confines of the family. The family is a miniature world of its own, a boot camp designed to equip its members for survival in the jungles of simple and complex cultures. If parenthood crumbles, society crumbles with it.

A GOD-GIVEN POSITION

We parents are finite individuals, novices, plagued by inconsistencies and imperfections. In spite of this, or better, because of this, parenthood has been elevated to an exalted status, not because it has earned it but because it cannot earn it. Parenthood is given a prominence of honor in society and woe unto us who ignore or underestimate this God-given position. It isn't earned, it cannot possibly be a reward for good behavior; it is a gift.

If this is the case, how is this honor perpetuated? The wisdom of Providence is greater than our own. Ministers are sometimes reluctant to talk about child rearing because the imperfections of *preachers' kids* are so conspicuous. Psychologists are sometimes experts in child psychology except at home. It is true that the cobbler's children wear unmended shoes; the baker's dozen have potatoes to eat but not cookies, etc. If we were to rely on parenthood to actually earn its respectability, a millennium might come and go.

Those of us who are parents must be made aware of the honorable position of parenthood. When this is accomplished we pass it on to the next generation by impressing upon our children the regality of parenthood. In effect, parents are king and queen of the home. Kings and queens have a tremendous responsibility for their subjects. This, among other things, includes their comfort and safety, nurture in education, religion, culture, and social life, as well as the many reciprocal relationships and responsibilities necessary for the preservation of the kingdom. The same holds true for the family.

We teach children to respect parents; in the process they learn to respect adults. We teach them to respect the home; in the process they learn to respect property. We teach them to respect brothers and sisters, neighbors, and values. If they cheat and steal or fight and curse, we deal with that in the home. Dad refuses to tolerate disrespect for Mom; Mom takes care not to undermine Dad's authority. The Bible is used as a model, the church is interwoven naturally into the fabric of daily life and, with it, eternal principles are passed from one generation to another. Big brothers exert a powerful influence on little brothers, supplementing the efforts of a godly father. Mother insists on manners and etiquette and teaches little girls to become refined young ladies. This cannot be accomplished nearly as effectively outside the home, if at all. Parenting holds an extremely unique role in society; parenthood is as honorable as we allow it to be.

Amazingly, the human infant is extremely vulnerable. Most animals can survive quite well apart from their parenting. Infants, on the other hand, are totally dependent upon adults. Children left on their own, not only physically but emotionally, will not thrive as human beings. God ordained it this way. For many years children need parenting—emotionally, mentally, physically, socially, spiritually. We shudder at what happens to infants left in seclusion or to children deprived of love and affection. Solitary confinement is cruel and inhuman, and no child should be exposed to it.

On the other hand we know also the tragedies that occur when children are pampered; undisciplined children become a menace to society; love-starved teenagers often manage to find some unwholesome activity to nourish their hunger. Children brought up by irresponsible parents usually become irresponsible people, and the converse is equally true. Unless children have instilled in them a high regard for parents, they are not apt to consider parenthood very favorably.

PERPETUATING THE ROLE

So far, we have been thinking of this relationship on a parent-child level. If a parent is convinced that parenthood is honorable, and behaves accordingly, it will not be discarded at any juncture in life. Children taught by parents that parenthood is a worthy profession will not only teach their children the same but will maintain an ongoing respect.

It is highly unlikely, for instance, that parents with a tenure of twenty-five years, having raised a family of respectable and respectful children, will forget the role their parents played in their lives. After all, it was their parents who created the legacy which in turn was passed on to the next generation. Now as their own parents approach retirement with its own peculiar and perplexing dimensions, parenthood still retains its regality. They can no more shrug off the needs of their parents any more than they can abandon the concerns of their children who are facing parenthood themselves.

Consequently, a middle-aged father takes his eldest, married daughter into his arms and reassures her that she will be a marvelous mother. Then he gets on the phone and tells his aging father that he's giving a week of his vacation to help him get his retirement feet on the ground. Parent-child relationships never end. Physically perhaps, but spiritually, emotionally, morally, never. This is divine: Honor your father and your mother. We instill it into our children from infancy until they are on their own. We render it unto our own parents until we bid them final farewell. This continues as our children look in on us in our old age, as we peeked in on them in their infancy. Parenthood is not only an honorable estate, it is an unending, unbroken circle.

PARENTHOOD IS COSTLY

As with everything worthwhile, parenthood is costly. If we were to count the costs of bringing a little one into the world and seeing that the necessities and a few luxuries of life were included, we would be astounded. In plain economics, the figure would be staggering. In terms of energy, the ergs would be unbelievable. In fact, we might find it impossible to believe that we actually were able to do it. But we did.

Along the way, however, little foxes gnawed at the vines. Children, often ingenious little con artists, sometimes manipulate far more than their share, often at the expense of someone else. Parents, either wearing blinders or actually myopic, sometimes play the awful game of favoritism, a contest in which there are no winners.

These and countless other maladies occur at every level. Parents too can become con artists, imposing their wills on reluctant or passive children. Middle-aged people sometimes prefer to pick up the tab for someone else to care for their elderly parents rather than expend time or energy themselves. The implications of this commandment are enormous, and if taken seriously, pose dimensions difficult to fathom.

Critical problems arise not only in child abuse but parental abuse as well, because parenthood has not been given its royal decree. To suddenly rearrange furniture to make room for an aging parent because of guilt or demand may be too great an adjustment. To spoil a child and suddenly begin a despoiling process could become disastrous. Yet, this happens every day.

There are times when it is perhaps better for parents to live in a retirement center than to be thrust into the boiling cauldron of one of their children. There are times when it may be best to gradually retrain a pampered child rather than suddenly take away accustomed indulgences. Common sense must rule, especially when principles outlined in the Decalogue have been ignored or disregarded over a period of time. Even so, these principles must somehow be reinstated or a generation or two may pass. That no society can afford.

KING OF THE FAMILY

In returning to the analogy of a mother-father as king and queen, we must rid ourselves of any negative imagery of a ruthless king and a conniving queen. The expression *honor*, denoting regality, must be honorable. Therefore, the father who is king of the family must behave in a kingly fashion. He is in charge; if not, his subjects detect the weakness and before long his kingdom will be in shambles. When he is in charge he should be a benevolent leader, not a cruel, ruthless, domineering, unreasonable tyrant.

A king normally has been trained by his father to assume the throne. Ideally he has been tutored adequately so that he is learned; he has been disciplined thoroughly so that he can both give and take orders; he has been conditioned so that he can work long hours when necessary and rule with a firm hand when circumstances demand it. He has been exposed to the finer aspects of life and is at home in the concert hall, the dining room, or in an art gallery. The crown prince, a king-in-training, has not been pampered or abused. He is chastened when he rebels and raised when he excels. He is given the rudiments of the military (kings are responsible for the safety of their subjects) and is well versed in the fundamentals of his religion.

A prospective father, likewise, should be trained by his father because someday he too will ascend the throne of parenthood. He should be tutored adequately and disciplined thoroughly in order to be able to give and take orders. The apprentice father should be conditioned to work, exposed to the finer aspects of life and should neither be pampered nor abused. The father-in-training must be adequately trained or the dynasty is liable to be broken.

When the writer of Proverbs wrote: *Train up a child in the way he ought to go*, he didn't stop there. He continued: *Then, when he matures, he will not forget what his training has accomplished* (paraphrased from Proverbs 22:6). Some interpret this to mean that a child may drift away from his or her upbringing but will return to it in old age. This may be. Many youth kick their heels for a while and seemingly get it out of their systems. There is, however, a better understanding. The key is found in the word *train*.

A wise king *trains* his son; a wise father *trains* his son. Unwise kings and fathers raise, perhaps, but do not train their children. Training involves far more than a casual upbringing. A parallel can be seen in what is involved in the training of an athlete or a musician. Hours and hours of drills, practice, exercises. Repetition. Repetition. Repetition. Review, correction, practice . . . review, correction, practice. At times it is painful, sheer agony, exhaustion. Then come the rewards: the sounds of praise, the celebrations, the thrill of spectators and the sense of achievement. *Training*. What a word. But that's the name of the game.

Within the family, and to a lesser degree perhaps than mentioned above, *training* is the key. The law, including the commandments, was to be written on the doorposts and drilled day and night until it was not only memorized but absorbed. Then, explanations of the law were to be given. Why tell a child, *Do not steal*, and not say why it is wrong? The casual approach to rearing a child is inadequate.

A wise mother likewise prepares her daughter for motherhood. Playing with dolls is an important role in bringing out the *motherly instinct* (if we dare express it this way). As the daughter matures she is taught over and over again the essential ingredients of being a woman and a mother. She is familiarized with the laundry as well as the kitchen, exposed frequently to the niceties of etiquette, glamour and aesthetics. Moral virtues and spiritual insights are taught as naturally as possible. By the time she reaches womanhood, motherhood is neither abhorred nor feared. When she takes her place in the home, she is not only wife and mother, she is a queen, ruling in her own right, transforming the home from a house to a castle. *Train up* a child, a son to become *king*, a daughter to become *queen*, and the whole world will rise in adoration and thanksgiving. Not only that, the world will survive and prosper. Ideally, a king and queen concept is complementary, not competitive.

Since the analogy of a crown prince-king relationship was used to illustrate but not exhaust the role of father and son and, to a lesser degree, the role of princess (daughter) and queen (mother), a further word is necessary. A good relationship between mothers and sons as well as between daughters and fathers is also essential. This is necessary in the development of healthy identities of the role of male and female as well as in other dimensions of human existence. For a single parent to be both father and mother to a child is impossible. Many single parents, however, when aware of this mother-father need in their children, do compensate in remarkable ways. With countless neighbors and friends, siblings and cousins, parents and in-laws available, it is not generally necessary that a child be deprived of masculine or feminine contacts. We must remember, however, that this commandment is dealing with normal mother and father roles, but not at the expense of single parent or non-extended family situations.

FOR STUDY OR DISCUSSION

1. With so many philosophies and books available on raising children, why is the Ten Commandment approach so necessary?

2. How reliable is common sense? One author titled his book *Holy Common Sense*. Does this make sense? How?

3. How does the word *honor* affect this commandment? Could we substitute a word such as *love, cherish,* or *obey*?

4. Is this statement valid: "As the family goes, so goes society"?

5. How can a single parent or a couple impress the regality of parenthood on the next generation?

6. Belongingness and security are vital to a child. How can these be accomplished? How long do they take? Can they be overdone?

7. What does this mean: Parenthood is an unending, unbroken circle?

8. What are the most common maladies that plague parenthood?

9. What is the difference between *raising* a child and *training* a child?

Chapter Six
SANCTITY

You shall not kill
Exodus 20:13

I am come that they might
have life, and that they might
have it more abundantly
(John 10:10, *KJV*).

A family in northern Minnesota had planned carefully for two years so that they could buy a snowmobile. Early in December they gave themselves their Christmas present. The ice looked so inviting, and some of it was already six inches thick. But in the middle of the lake ice hadn't formed yet; the water was open, black and cold. The father revved the brand new engine, listened to it purr, took a spin around the house. Then everyone—Mom, Dad, and the three kids—climbed aboard. An hour later their neighbor saw them sailing across the ice, the same ice they knew was too dangerous to even consider. But there they were, all five of them. A few moments later all was quiet. The ice had yawned and swallowed them. Death can be so cold, so tragic, so merciless. And so final.

In an immaculate hospital lay the mother of five small children. At one time she was a beautiful woman, a charming person, a model mother. For months disease had declared war on her body, but she wouldn't give up. Her body had almost wasted away, her voice had lost its ring, her eyes had grown dim and although her little ones called, she could barely hear them. When she did hear she couldn't answer. One evening, with her family at her side, she closed her eyes for the last time and quietly slipped away. There were tears, many of them, but they were tears of thanksgiving as well as sorrow. They knew she was going on a long journey, and they knew where she was going—to a land where there is no pain, no sorrow, no suffering. Death can also be a blessing.

When the vertical relationships between God and His people break down, it's only a matter of time before the horizontal relationships (people to people) are affected. The ancient Israelites discovered this in their tribal existence en route from Egypt to Palestine. We are told that they began to grumble about the food and the water. What manna was like we can only speculate; it probably was quite tasty. But seven days a week, week after week? Even steak loses its appeal after successive days, believe it or not.

When things go wrong a scapegoat is a handy commodity. At first the people complained about weather; then it was the water; the next was about manna. Someone had to be blamed, and Moses became the scapegoat. But ultimately, God got the blame.

When a civilization, or a nation comprising a dozen tribes, or a country with fifty states or forty provinces, begins to lose its divine sensitivity, inhumanity toward humanity follows. The tribes of Israel had slowly, it seems, degenerated under the heat of the Sinai sun. But was it the sun, the water, and the manna, or the absence of leeks and onions? Probably not. The people had lost their sensitivity, their sense of appreciation, their respect for each other as well as their leaders, their religion and their deity.

When this happens, people tend to become less than people. They act like animals or incompetents. Their conscience takes a beating and human life no longer is sacred. Murder, unthought of before, is defended as justifiable homicide. Unwanted children are sacrificed, if not to awaiting arms of colossal idols or yawning furnaces, then to anonymous graves or unmarked crevices. Even wanted children could be sacrificed if the insensitivity were great enough. A stealing neighbor would be hunted as an animal. Revenge was a human occupation resulting in an eye for an eye, a life for a life.

Cities of refuge were established for innocents (and possibly some with just cause). Life, which for generations had probably been highly regarded, suddenly was cheap. It is almost incongruous that God would have to include this tough axiom in His moral law: YOU SHALL NOT MURDER. But evidently even His chosen people warranted this dictum as they fell apart morally. Somewhere, somehow, the law of sensitivity written on the heart had been obscured. Now it was rechiseled in granite—and there it remains—indelible.

The Decalogue is now dealing with some of the nitty-gritty aspects of person-to-person relationships. The best place to begin is where the sixth commandment begins—life is sacred. Life is eternal. Life is worth living. A popular psychologist insists that only the insane want to die. I think he is right. Self-preservation is built in, one of the strongest drives we have. We do want to live, we want to live well, and we want to live forever. Since the Creator designed us this way, He was obligated to make certain that we do not forget. Therefore, this commandment.

You shall not kill more correctly means not to murder. That is, we are not to put another person to death intentionally and unlawfully, with premeditated or impulsive malice.

Within the body of a human being lives the soul. When the body ceases to function, the soul departs but it lives on. When God outlawed murder He was not primarily concerned with the body; He was protecting the home of the soul. An elderly physician once lectured to a group of clergymen. He stated that he believed every one has a soul. Having been at the bedside of innumerable patients when they died, he felt he could tell when the soul left the body. Some may scoff at this, but it does point up one of the great medical controversies: When does death occur? Does death occur when the major functions of the body cease; when the brain no longer is able to function; when the heart and pulse lie silent? Or, is it when the soul leaves the body?

Life is the greatest possession a person has. Not only is it strategic while he lives, it is the passport to life after death. No greater thing can one do than lay down one's life for another. This is what makes Christianity unique: Jesus gave His life that we might live. We came into the world to live; He came to die. The world is full of those who want to be heroes without heroics, martyrs without martyrdom. We hang on to our lives with a fierce tenacity while often failing to value the lives of others. I wept as I read about some fourteen-year-old boys who stole a car. Before long they abandoned it and fled into a flooded river bed. Hours later, a search party heard cries and rescued two of them. One was hanging onto a branch in the swollen waters, shivering in the cold; with the other hand he was clutching his pal. How long he had been hanging on we don't know, but it wasn't until he was rescued that he found out his pal was dead. Had he known, would he have let him go?

YOU SHALL NOT MURDER

Basically, this commandment outlaws murder. Murder can be a savage revenge and it can be a shrewd manipulation of human life. Murder can be singular or plural. This commandment was not written merely for a semi-literate primitive who had no sense of human dignity; it was written for the jealous, bitter Cain, yes, but it was also written for the diabolical David who put a husband into the thick of battle, knowing he would be killed, so that he could "legitimately" commit adultery. Murder can be subtle, it can be hidden from the eyes of the law, and it can be made to look like an accident or a death from natural causes; but murder is murder.

The whole aspect of death, killing, murder, mercy killing, suicide, and abortion must be seriously questioned by parents. We must answer the hard questions about war and suicide, euthanasia and abortion as they relate to the sacredness of human life.

Why is human life so sacred? A human differs from an animal, although some say humans are the highest form of animal life. No other creation of the Creator has surpassed *Homo sapi-*

ens. The human being is God's crowning achievement. When we humans were created, the universe gave God a standing ovation. God made us in His own image and likeness; we are living souls. In fact, Adam was told to name the animals, to use them for his needs for food, as servants, for transportation, as pets . . . . Although animals have certain powers that far surpass similar dimensions of humans, animals are inferior.

Humans have the ability to think abstractly; we have the capacity to reason, to reflect, to rationalize. A beaver can build a dam and an eagle a nest, but no animal has ever built a computer. Man creates not only what he needs, but what he wants: a bridge, a dam, an airplane, a school, a slide trombone, a computer.

Humans have both the desire and the ability to worship. An elephant can be taught to stand on one leg on top of a block, but no elephant has ever prayed; no beaver has ever built a cathedral. A dog knows shame but cannot say, "I'm sorry." There is something within causing us to reach out for someone greater than ourselves. God therefore has decreed that no one shall cut another life short lest this privilege be denied.

We are able to develop language skills. We are able to converse at a very elementary level as well as in depth. Animals communicate, but not at this level. We interpret abstract symbols and translate them into meaningful concepts, a dimension no other creation possesses.

For these reasons and others, God has ordained that we are fearfully and wonderfully made, created in the image of our Creator Himself. No wonder we are sacred beings, worthy of the priceless possession of life.

GOD IS A HOLY GOD

The next dimension we must examine is this: If God outlawed murder, why did He allow His people to be such a warlike nation? Joy Davidman has expressed this concept rather bluntly in her volume *Smoke on the Mountain*:

How the ancient Jews did slaughter! They killed in hot blood, and cold; they killed for loot, for God, and for fun. To spare prisoners of war and their women and children was considered almost blasphemy. "Go and utterly destroy the sinners!" says the Lord to Saul, and when the warrior king tries to spare Agag, the priest and prophet Samuel defends religion by chopping the helpless captive to bits. "Sun, stand thou still upon Gibeon," commands Joshua, lest the killing might have to stop. Nor was war the only form of pastime. The tribes killed by trickery and riotous massacre, as in The Book of Esther; by wholesale legal extermination, as when Joshua finished off Achan and his sons and daughters; by political assassination, as when Ehud stabbed King Eglon in his fat belly; by violation of hospitality, as when Jael knocked her tenpenny nail through the sleeping Sisera's brain; by treachery in love, as when Judith first seduced Holofernes and then sliced off his head . . . [These] were set down as tribal legends of the bad old days before the law, when the Jews were not people of the Book but marauding nomads rather like Sioux who finished off Custer at the Little Big Horn. And their value to us is largely as a grim picture of what all people are like before God speaks in the thunder on Sinai—or after they have forgotten what he said.[1]

Miss Davidman well represents many of the critics of Old Testament warriors. Abraham lived considerably before Moses smashed the tablets of stone on the sides of old Mount Sinai, but we would hardly call him primitive, nor would we consider the highly advanced civilization of Ur of the Chaldees backward. Joshua, Samuel, Esther and Jael—all mentioned by Miss Davidman—arrived on the scene after Moses lost his cool. They were hardly representative of the "bad old days before the law" although they do represent those who had forgotten what Moses had said. She is correct in saying that God's people did every imaginable cruel deed. They murdered, they killed in cold and hot blood, they seduced, assassinated, they exterminated—and yes, they literally committed genocide among the Canaanites.

Either God violated His own integrity in the "thunderstones" by ordering that which He condemned or we have misunderstood the situation. We must not forget that these same bloodthirsty Hebrews departed so far from God's grace that they too were destroyed.

God had repeatedly warned the Canaanite savages to repent of their iniquity or pay the consequences. Their civilization was so abominable, so inhuman (modern archeology bears this out) that God had to destroy them. Their cup of iniquity was full! God has destroyed by water, plague, pestilence, fire, and the sword and has warned of an eventual holocaust yet to come. Nations have destroyed themselves by dissipation, internal strife, economic absurdity, and gross debauchery.

Seldom is literature as candid as the Old Testament. It tells it as it is; chips fly in every direction; concealed motives are exposed. Because the Hebrews fought "dirty" does not mean that God approved. God weeps over the sins of men; He doesn't gloat! Those who live by the sword perish by the sword not because they are less savage but because they are more wicked. Sodom and Nineveh testify to both the compassion and intolerance of God.

In viewing the takeover of China and Russia, the tyranny of the infamous Hitler regime, the Koreas and Viet Nams, the fierce Arab-Israeli conflicts, and Irish and Lebanese civil strifes, Latin American and African crises, mankind seems not to have progressed very far since Sinai. Mankind has forgotten, if it ever learned, what God said to Moses long ago.

God is a God of love, but He is also a holy God, a God of justice as well as mercy, a jealous, terrible, awesome, compassionate deity. God wills that no man shall perish. He cringes every time a sword pierces the heart of His noblest creation. To make God one thing in the Old Testament and another in the New is bad theology; God is immutable (changeless). But God cannot allow the godless to hinder the way of the godly. Even though the Hebrews did not measure up to God's standards, they were His chosen people through which would come His ultimate salvation. Therefore God allowed them to carry out

His judgment and punishment upon the wicked. But the people didn't stop there. Blatant evil, treachery, crime, and an inhumane *lex talionis*—an eye for an eye and a tooth for a tooth—resulted in spite of God's decree, *You shall not kill*.

GO THE SECOND MILE

It could be rather easy to make this commandment less than what it was meant to be. There is a positive aspect to it as well: Not only should a person commit no murder, he should "go the second mile." With mass communications stressing the tragic, the bizarre—murders and plane crashes always get front-page coverage—there is the danger of losing the capacity to become shocked. We tend to react emotionally when someone we know is involved, but if an explosion in a mine buries half a hundred miners, we tend to be less sensitive than we would like to be (or ought to be). Elton Trueblood (*Foundations for Reconstruction*) wrote about the necessity of "cultivating an uneasy conscience." When our capacity to feel with and for others wanes, we must do something about it.

It is possible to be overly sensitive to the needs and wants of those around us, even to the point where we disrupt normal existence. Somewhere between these two extremes—overly sensitive versus insensitive—is a better way. This commandment prohibits murder but goes far beyond.

One of the finest ways of upholding this commandment is building a home where parents stress the dignity and sanctity of human life—that everyone regardless of race, color, or creed has a right to live, and to live at least reasonably well. Children also should be taught that many, unfortunately, do not share this high regard for human life and personal dignity. They will then understand why some people are poor, others are criminals, and at least a few are heartless. When a child understands that the human body is the "temple of the Holy Spirit," a temporary rooming house for the soul, and that the spirit is far more important than the body, he will be much better fortified for life.

We have been told that life ends when we draw our final

breath or when our soul departs. This is not so. Human existence, according to Scripture, is eternal. C.S. Lewis in *The Great Divorce* wrestles vigorously with life after death, depicting a journey by some of the occupants of hell who visit heaven. They found it intolerable and quickly returned "home." It is unthinkable that God would force those who couldn't tolerate Him on earth to spend eternity with Him. This is why (one of the reasons) God has prepared two separate abodes for life after death.

Logically it is also absurd to think that life ends in death. There are countless who die with little or no recognition of what they have done—good or evil. It is illogical and unbiblical to believe that a Hitler could establish such a regime and bark out such inhuman orders only to escape human and divine justice by merely taking his own life.

Thou shall not kill was not meant only for occupants of death row, it is aimed at every living soul, reminding us that life is precious, eternal, sacred—the greatest possession we have. God forbids that any tamper with the life of another. May God help us sustain life and nurture it—socially, mentally, physically and spiritually.

THE SANCTITY OF HUMAN LIFE

The taking of another man's life is always unfortunate. At times it may be impossible to avoid. Accidents do occur; self-defense has resulted in death; war has sometimes been a "necessary evil"; police at times must shoot to kill. Criminals have been put to death for their crimes. Incurable patients have often been artificially kept alive, living a slow death—others have mercifully been allowed to die. Soul-searching agony has wracked the minds of physicians forced to choose between a mother and her unborn. Men have been tortured, brainwashed, and stripped of that which makes them human. Children have been placed in solitary confinement emerging more animal-like than human. Life is terribly complicated and great demands are made on human reason. In fact, these demands are too great for the mortal mind.

That is why this command was etched in stone. The underlying principle behind every act of man, every decision regarding our fellowman, is deeply rooted in this command. In every situation the sanctity of human life must dominate every action. For instance, war could conceivably be justified by society to stop an injustice when all other means have failed. But when this principle is violated, war is not only hell, it is wrong.

A father had a son who was the smallest lad in his grade. The classroom bully delighted in harassing this defenseless lad. The father, a compassionate man with no animosity or hatred, tried to negotiate a settlement with the bully: he talked kindly to him, reasoned with the other father, discussed it with his son's teacher, invited the bully to his home and introduced him to his hobby (antique cars), discussed the situation with the peer leaders of the classroom. All of this failed, and his son was still the victim of a great deal of physical abuse. As a last resort, the father taught his son karate. When the boy was ready the father gave his son permission to settle the issue when the opportune moment arose. The next day the bully lost his bullishness—in a hurry. The father was wiser than many of us. The son went the second mile attempting to win the friendship of the bully—which he did.

At times, war may be the only way out. People get so bullish they will not negotiate; they will not reason; they will not relent. Strange as it may sound, could it be wrong at times not to wage war? Hitler had to be stopped, and although an all-out war might have been a little hasty according to some critics, it came almost too late. Even in war, the sanctity of human existence must be the guiding principle. Unfortunately, many hawks and doves alike have failed to be led by this guiding light—*life is sacred*. War is hell—ask anyone who has been there. Many of us are unaware of the horrible decisions commanding officers must face in dealing with self-defense, enemy tactics and preemptive methods. What would we do if we knew that withdrawing military forces from a nation would result in a wholesale massacre? How would we react if an enemy brutally ravished our women and children? Human life is sacred, and those who disregard life—friend or foe—are violating an eternal principle.

We live in a world where the white man is rapidly becoming a member of a significant, but hopelessly outnumbered, minority race. Black and yellow people far overshadow the white, and no longer is the white man the prima donna of the universe. In all probability he never was, although western civilization has triumphed gloriously in many ways. Even so, the racial tensions plaguing our shrinking globe will never be resolved until this utterance of the Decalogue is taken seriously. In God's sight, all are created equal—not identical and in many cases not even similar, but equal—red and white, black and yellow are created in the image and likeness of God. Behind the skin lies a soul, and within that soul beats the heart of a human. Whenever mankind forgets this there will be no end of strife. The war of words resulting from the war of nerves often leads to the battlefield. The white cannot give the black any rights or vice versa; these were given to everyone everywhere by the Creator and reinforced by the sixth commandment.

Also condemned in the sixth command is human injustice of every kind. It condemns landed gentry who treat slaves as human cultivators. It condemns landlords who treat tenants worse than rodents. It condemns mine owners who use men as mules, and suave extortionists who rob widows and the aged, the pimp who sells young damsels into prostitution. It condemns the father who makes his own rules, the minister who preaches his own doctrine, the mother who fails to teach her children . . . . Scripture is clear. God is a no-nonsense God. Those who think they have hoodwinked the Almighty will some day find themselves on bended knees.

DISCUSSION SITUATIONS

Life and death are crucial concerns for the family. The child who has been taught that every one is precious in the sight of God has been done a great favor. He may never come to realize this; or he may have to learn it the hard way. There are several terms that every family must grapple with sooner or later in the matters of human dignity, the sanctity of the soul, eternal life, death, and a host of other matters. The following subject areas, among others, parents ought to take time to discuss in depth with their children. A sensitive, warm approach based upon the principles of God's "blueprint" in dealing with the *sanctity* of human life will save considerable anguish later on. Opportunities often present themselves naturally; a family rarely has to create discussion situations, although at times it is necessary.

The following subjects will not be treated in depth; they are only a beginning point for parents and children to struggle with together. Hopefully, as parent and child dialogue on these and other subjects a mature, proper attitude toward human life will unfold.

ABNORMALITY—Disruptions of the human body can occur in almost any phase of development—before, during, and following birth. Each situation is unique and must be handled on the basis of its own particularities. Excessive pity and attention may smother a handicapped child, causing more suffering as well as afflicting other members of the family. The opposite is also true. God, who designed the human body, has allowed nature to run its course. Therefore, there are malfunctions. These are not willed by God as punishment, nor does the Almighty guarantee that a miracle will take place. God has promised, though, to give strength and wisdom for the hour, and many in adversity are made strong. Many lovely souls have dwelled within defective bodies. It might be trite, but it's still true—a deficiency can be a blessing in disguise.

ABORTION—Although most parents do not discuss abortion with small children, a time will come when the subject will arise along with birth control and sexual activity among peers. The whole subject of abortion on demand for the promiscuous to therapeutic abortion for victims of rape should be carefully analyzed. This is closely akin to the question of when life begins (conception or birth or . . . ?) and the awesome responsibility involved in giving birth and subsequent parenting. There are no easy answers to abortion but there are governing principles that directly or indirectly speak to this subject. (For consideration read Psalm 139:13-16 and Jeremiah 1:5 when considering life before birth.)

BIRTH—We kid a lot about the "birds and the bees" but often that's all we do. The church, school, and neighborhood have often taken over for home. Sex education has had both beneficial and harmful effects. Birth is still a miraculous mystery, a "blessed event." At times it is ill-timed; siblings sometimes take a pretty dim view of an *intruder*. When birth occurs, parents and children alike need to be prepared well in advance. This can be a momentous experience, spiritually meaningful; and it can be a negative experience. Birth leads eventually to subsidiary subjects such as abortion, masturbation, miscarriage, birth control, and other premarital inquiries. If parents are able to talk sensitively and openly about sex to their own children, it will be relatively easy to discuss other intimate subjects as they arise. With this in mind, wise parents should take the subject of sex education seriously, beginning early and continuing throughout the developing stages of the chid.

CAPITAL PUNISHMENT—Punitive action can range from a bitter retaliation to an attempt to discourage further criminality. Authorities disagree on the remedy for crime, and many argue over the morality of taking another's life regardless of the crime. This debate will not soon be settled; in fact, future generations may reverse some prevailing notions. To argue that capital punishment is always commanded by Scripture is illogical. As previously pointed out the *lex talionis* (an eye for an eye . . .) was allowed because of the hardness of the hearts of the people. It never was intended to supercede the sixth commandment. It was also intended to restrain humankind so that a life would not be taken for a limb. We are disturbed when a youth commits suicide in his jail cell after six weeks of near solitary confinement; we are also disturbed when a hard-core, dangerous criminal lurks in the shadows because he was set free on a technicality. This is a subject parents dare not avoid, seeking biblical as well as civil answers.

CRUELTY—Kindness and compassion are best taught early in life. When a child abuses his mother, Dad better step in; when a child is mean to an animal, an excellent learning situation is established. Human life is sacred; therefore cruelty in any form is intolerable, and cruelty of any kind can be used as a springboard to teach sensitivity.

DEATH—Civilized man does everything possible to maintain life, partly because death is so final. The Christian parent is able to view death as a blessing, a reward, a promotion, a natural phenomenon. The moment a child is born he begins to die. Tragic, untimely, soul-searching deaths pose enormous difficulties for even Christian parents who do not despair but who do sorrow greatly. The Christian parent also must bid farewell to friends and relatives who made no claim to being believers. Death always brings up the subject of heaven and hell, paradise and purgatory; it will sooner or later evoke questions regarding reincarnation, communication with the dead, soul sleep, annihilation and universalism, last rites and baptism for the dead. If life were but a fleeting moment, a bubble soon to burst, a vapor that will vanish beneath the warm rays of the sun, then why all the fuss about death and life after death?

ETERNITY—The Scripture states that all have everlasting life. Scripture tells us that this eternal life—eternal in the sense of everlasting, not in the divine sense of having no beginning—is determined by what we do with the Messiah. If we take the Bible as our final authority we are not overwhelmed by the fact that we are living, eternal souls. This is beyond our comprehension and imagination; that is why God has placed the thought (the conception, the very idea) of eternity in our mind. This is another reason why we are to treat human life with sanctity.

FATE—Some are fatalists believing that all events are determined by fate and are therefore inevitable. Others have a rather flimsy grasp of providentialism and our relationship to an omniscient God. To blame God for all the events of nature and society is just as bad as saying that what is meant to be will be.

How we regard human life depends upon our theology. With little difficulty we can turn God into an extremely naive, permissive being or into a razor-sharp hatchet man separating the elite from the damned. As parents, we have an obligation to be theologically astute, answering questions with logic and wisdom, but also with biblical perspective.

KILLING—Some interpret this command to prohibit all killing—man, beast, fowl, insect. Man was told to subdue the earth; fish and fowl, beast and insect have been provided for his enrichment as well as survival. By its spirit the commandment does prohibit cruelty to animals, and wanton destruction of anything is evil. Without doubt, killing should be avoided if at all possible when it involves humanity. There are times when killing may be unavoidable (war, law, self-defense, accidental); even then, killing could be murder and should be judged accordingly. For instance, a policeman could shoot but be so full of hatred that he shoots not only to keep from being shot but to destroy wantonly. Killing is a complex issue and cannot be understood or evaluated apart from a divine ruling; therefore the Decalogue.

MERCY KILLING—There are times when a person begs for death due to a hopelessly incurable disease or extreme pain, or he may be starving to death with no hope of rescue or sustenance. Is it ever right to allow a person to die when the situation is hopeless? Is it ever right to prolong the life of a person when there is no hope (humanly speaking)? Euthanasia is a complicated question and must be considered in depth. The spirit of the command as well as the letter of the law must be understood.

MURDER—There are several overtones of this word that should be considered: (1) the unlawful killing of another person with malice aforethought; (2) to kill inhumanly or barbarously; (3) to eliminate another person, not necessarily with malice aforethought, but with the intent to gain something in exchange for his removal; (4) to mar or injure another person without killing him. The spirit of this commandment sought to condemn all these aspects when it declared, *You shall not mur-*

der. Murder and killing can be two different things; yet they can be identical. We will do well to know the distinction.

SANCTITY—We are holy, sacred, hallowed beings—handle with care! There is also another dimension: a blinding force. We are related (bound) to our Creator making us extra special in the eyes of the universe. This sanctity of man is to be regarded as inviolable. Because we are humans, not animals, and because life is eternal, not temporal, life is sacred.

SUICIDE—The intentional taking of one's own life claims an unknown number of lives everywhere. How many suicides there are that appear to be accidental or natural deaths, or covered up intentionally in some way, no one will ever know. God has put the drive of self-preservation within us for a good reason: it keeps us going when the going gets rough; it enables us to love our neighbor as we love ourselves (self-esteem and self-respect, not an egotistical or morbid self-love); it helps us shoulder the burdens of other human beings; it gives us a hope for the tomorrow; it gives us a chance to atone for a sin or mistake or bad judgment. Taking our own life short-circuits any hope or second chance since death is the immediate gateway from life to *life after death*. This sixth commandment—by implication—applies to suicide as well as murder. It is important that children learn these distinctions.

WAR—*Peace at any price* is dangerous business; so is being trigger-happy. The Bible predicts that there will always be war and rumors of war. Statisticians and historians have analyzed past civilizations and found very few blocks of history free of turmoil and conflict. Although we should never accept a defeatist attitude of a hawkish, warmongering mania, neither should we underestimate the nature of mankind. Civilized nations fight more sophisticatedly perhaps, but no less realistically than primitive tribes. Education, prosperity, and technology have not stopped war, nor have the finest parents been able to handle every squabble between siblings. War is here to stay; it's inevitable and will be abolished only in the Kingdom yet to come. To work for its abolition is one thing; to underestimate the depravity of man is another.

In the light of these and other critical matters, there must be a guiding principle going before us wherever we journey: we are the inspiration of a holy God, made in His likeness and image, with such a premium placed on our heads that no one dare harm us in any way without God's consent or reprisal. Human life is sacred. Without a high regard for human life, life becomes cheap, expendable, and eventually meaningless. However, maintaining life is not enough. Jesus came not only to give eternal life, but to enrich our daily existence. Without Him, life is never what it was intended to be.

FOR STUDY OR DISCUSSION

1. Discuss the *tragedy* and *triumph* of death.
2. What is the distinction between *killing* and *murdering*?
3. Why is human life sacred?
4. The Old Testament is riddled with "blood and guts." In fact, at times it is brutally candid, but so is everyday life. Why is the O.T. so candid?
5. If life is sacred, how does this affect our attitude toward abortion, capital punishment, euthanasia, suicide and war?
6. Discuss this adage: "All is fair in love and war."
7. What is the difference between the "first resort" and the "last resort"? Give some illustration of this.
8. The home (dinner table, a TV program, bedtime, travel, conversation, etc.) is a natural place to get involved in matters of the sacredness of life. Give examples of how this has worked (or not worked) in your situation.
9. How can a parent become theologically astute as well as humanly sensitive?
10. Revering life and maintaining it is not enough. What more is demanded of us?

Note

1. Joy Davidman, *Smoke on the Mountain: An Interpretation of the Ten Commandments* (Philadelphia: Westminster Press, 1970).

Chapter Seven

FIDELITY

You shall not commit adultery
Exodus 20:14

What therefore God has
joined together, let not man
put asunder (Matt. 19:6).

Marital fidelity in Judeo-Christian circles was far more important years ago than today. Today, even in Christian surroundings, extramarital sex is not only practiced, it is sometimes defended.

When the Israelites lived in Egypt they were exposed to neighbors who had no highly developed concept of fidelity. In fact, by the time of the New Testament, Jewish standards seemed to be somewhat skewed, evidenced by the woman caught in the act of adultery. She was seemingly guilty but not the other party. Why, going back some centuries, should David have several wives but Ruth seemingly could have but one husband?

This commandment is ingenious in that it is no discerner of persons. It matters not the sex or the station in life. Adultery is prohibited, period. "Justifiable adultery" was never tolerated. Arguing in a sense from silence, the fact that this seventh principle was chiseled into stone implies that adultery existed.

As the tribes set up camp, the proximity of one tent to another invited hanky-panky. The loneliness of the journey, the emptiness of the soul out of harmony with its Creator, the commonplace of infidelity among their neighbors, the disillusionment with their leaders coupled with the appeal of the forbidden, all helped to introduce adultery to these wanderers. Infidelity can be habit-forming. Once the threshold of fidelity is crossed, subsequent journeys can be made with relative ease.

It is probably safe to say that adulterous relationships occur, not necessarily due to marital distress or dissatisfaction, but because spiritual relationships have dimmed, God is not taken seriously, parents have not instilled values and respect into children, and because the conscience has been anesthetized. When the divine becomes commonplace, and when the commonplace becomes deified, loyalty and fidelity, commitment and chastity are short-circuited. Adultery is not the result of marital failure; it is the result of a disregard for the first six commandments. Even so-called weak or perilous marriages can survive the onslaught of adultery or infidelity if priorities and sensitivities are in order.

Whatever the cause, adultery had penetrated the nomadic tribes of Israel. Moses brought the terse word to his people: YOU SHALL NOT COMMIT ADULTERY. Ironically, Paul delivered the same message to the believers, especially in Rome and Corinth. Today, the same message is needed again.

Without a biblical view of human nature, the sex drive could well be considered simply another of the human drives needing gratification. It is painfully true that Christianity is frustrating to those who believe that sexual gratification is merely another of God's gifts to humankind. That it is, but it is infinitely more than a biological urge.

Since the Ten Commandments have a way of reinforcing one another, this divine dictum is specifically aimed at marriage rather than the broad aspects of human sexuality. Although amazing complexities do arise within the bonds of holy (and unholy) wedlock, fidelity is the name of the game. Without fidelity, marriage not only loses its luster, it loses its nature.

The ancient Hebrews, their wandering quest of the Promised Land, had seemingly deteriorated to such an extent that

Moses was compelled to speak out forcefully on the matter of fidelity. Because the matter was so critical God called Moses aside and indelibly inscribed this message on the face of a hard rock: YOU SHALL NOT COMMIT ADULTERY. It, unlike some other messages of the decalogue, was unqualified. There was no room for extenuating circumstances. The loopholes of an *if* or *unless* were closed.

The key to this command is found in the deliberate choice of the word *adultery*. Had the word *fornication* been used, this command would have been aimed at sexual abstinence outside wedlock rather than fidelity within. It is marriage that needs and is given divine protection.

Adultery must be defined. In its strictest sense, it means the willful violation of a marriage union by either partner engaging in sexual intercourse with a third party, married or otherwise. In a misguided sense, it implied a married woman engaging in an act of infidelity. Even today, in certain circles, there seems to be immunity given to a man but nowhere in biblical writ can this dual standard be defended. This is also seen in the pharisaical practice of non-virginal males seeking virgins for wives, and the practice of seduction through whimsy: *If you love me, you will*.

Juxtaposed against this is an unwritten law that a woman has considerable power at her disposal in establishing moral standards. Put another way, when a woman tumbles or leaps from her pedestal of fidelity, the whole earth feels the shock. Even so, it takes two to tangle, and it takes two to uphold fidelity. One cannot do it alone.

Fornication, on the other hand, might have been chosen to punctuate the seventh command, but it wasn't. If so, the command would have taken an entirely different slant. In defining fornication, a word not used regularly in normal conversation, it means any act of heterosexual intercourse outside the framework of marriage.

In other words a married person engaging in sexual intercourse with a third party, married or otherwise, is committing both fornication and adultery. However, two unmarried persons engaging in sexual intercourse are committing fornication but not adultery. Both adultery and fornication lie outside biblical bounds.

Ironically, this command stands counter not only to much of contemporary culture which so often condones or even encourages sexually active participation among consenting persons, it stood pretty much alone in biblical times as well. The Hebrews, to whom this was specifically addressed, were surrounded by peoples who not only encouraged sexual behavior but often incorporated it into the religious fabric of their cultures. Temple prostitution, male and female, is difficult for the modern mind to grasp, but perhaps no more difficult than for an ancient to understand the implicit (and explicit) sex pandemic of the twentieth century.

To our Creator, marriage is something special. It is worth having, and it is worth keeping. Marriage, in the biblical sense, is the fusion of two persons into one flesh, a divine union of body, soul, and mind. To suggest that marriage is a human invention is to err. *Marriage was conceived in heaven* although *marriages are made on earth*. When God instituted marriage He had human nature in mind. Marriage is more than a ceremonial procedure; it is more than a licensing process; it is even more than a covenant or a pact or even a human fusion of two mutually consenting persons; it is God at His creative best.

The word *asunder* is another non-everyday expression. Literally, it means to tear apart. Marriage, in God's mind, is a divine fusion of two bodies and minds which can only be torn apart with considerable pain. Adultery is not a mere human obduracy; it is tampering with an act of God.

This divine fusion, regrettably, has been cheapened considerably. Sexual intercourse is hardly limited to married persons although it was intended that way from the beginning. Because of its being made so commonplace, it is difficult for many to comprehend what God had in mind with this physical act being the final and most noble aspect of the consummation of two individuals committed eternally to each other. In fact, it is almost a sacrament, and in some arenas of Christendom, marriage is sacramental. Although this point could be debated, let it suffice to say that marriage is not merely a ceremony which takes away the guilt of sexual intercourse. To the contrary, many varying studies seem to indicate that there is considerable anxiety, guilt, fear, pain and dissatisfaction with sexual intercourse within marriage, even marriages of rather long standing. As with the art of marriage itself (and marriage is an art), sexual intercourse takes time, tenderness, understanding, energy, cooperation, and even considerable mutual experience before it begins to achieve perfection. Evidently this is too high a price to pay, at least for many couples. It appears to be easier and more alluring to start over with another partner. This is another reason society kids itself, thinking that clandestine affairs are satisfying. Even so-called *innocent* affairs cannot, at best, deliver much more than physical gratification.

Sexual intercourse, at its best, is much more spiritual ecstasy than biological. Its physical climax, rated so highly in many circles, is important, but only as a means, not as an end. To many it seems to be primarily a biological, physiological function but the Creator had something much more noble in mind.

This commandment is terse. It flatly forbids adultery. Why? Because adultery is always painful? Not always. We all know the adage that *stolen kisses are the sweetest*. There is something about the forbidden that makes it tantalizing. God no doubt also had this in mind when He chiseled the rock on Mount Sinai. No adultery! Not even if your spouse is cheating on you. Not even if you were caught in a depressing moment. Not even if you were titillated by a seductive neighbor (or a stranger). We argue, rationalize, and attempt to justify at least some forms of adultery; but in God's plan it is futile. Adultery is crossing the threshold of the forbidden. Once crossed, it can be crossed repeatedly. For some, this can be an exhilarating, triumphant experience; for others, it can be so traumatic that any hope of reconciliation is shattered.

Adultery, in my judgment, is also forbidden because couples need this kind of admonition. Let me illustrate. My daughter, early one evening, asked me to tell her to be home by eleven o'clock. I caught the message and told my teenager to be in at eleven! She was going out with an unknown individual and wanted a safeguard, just in case. Couples also need this kind of safeguard. Couples are being bombarded with all kinds of marital advice including the urging to "play around a little" because "it is healthy for marriage." And not a few are falling for it. There are times when a person needs assurance that when the tempter comes, he or she can *head for home at eleven*. When it comes to adultery, God made it clear: DON'T! We don't even need to examine extenuating circumstances or question motives because they don't apply. It is not an either/or situation. If it were, we'd be wracking our brains to find excuses to engage in extramarital affairs which, regrettably, much of society seems to be doing.

God foresaw the twentieth century. We're told that in 1948, fewer than 20 percent of the nation's wives/mothers worked outside the home. Today it is approaching (or has passed) the 50 percent figure and still rising. This too has placed considerable strain on marriage. Coupled with changing social and ethical mores, the so-called sexual emancipation, the tragic breaking down of the family and an aggressive women's liberation mood, a casual, nonchalant, escape-hatch marital relationship is inadequate. When the pressure is great, why not run? Fidelity is the glue which can hold a union together; loyalty, camaraderie, love, understanding, encouragement, and togetherness, when given a chance, keep marriages from coming apart.

If a husband goes to the office day after day, takes a beating from the swingers because of his unwavering fidelity, gets bypassed for promotions because he is not a partying politician, he may begin to doubt his faith, and after a while may even question the sanctity of fidelity. But if he comes home to a wife who has tidied the house, put fresh flowers on the table, and dashes into his arms (in front of the gawking neighbors) to tell him that she loves him, fidelity somehow seems pretty good again.

But suppose he comes home to a dumpy, nagging spouse

who doesn't acknowledge his arrival, and when she speaks she tells him only the naughty things little Johnny did. Then fidelity dims and the new secretary looks better every day.

Or suppose a wife goes to the office, is admired by the male entourage for her secretarial skills as well as appearance, but comes home to her husband who got off at three and is glued to the TV set and barely grunts a hello. Fidelity, unfortunately, could begin to fade.

It is not the purpose of this commandment to define the role of husbands and wives, working at home or beyond; it is, however, concerned with the tensions, pressures, injustices, and temptations that occur to both husband and wife. Fidelity, loyalty, patience, understanding and love are superior virtues, far ahead of lesser attributes such as physical gratification, titillation, pleasure or revenge. Unless a marriage is built upon fidelity, and unless this fidelity is sustained by both husband and wife, any marriage will at least lean if not topple when the winds blow. And, like it or not, the winds will blow.

It may be well to pause at this point to suggest a converse: *Anything which contributes, directly or indirectly, to the breakdown of marriage must be examined carefully.* If a Christian or secular society encourages conditions which aggravate fidelity within marriage, the spirit of this seventh commandment is being undermined. For instance, the rising incidence of working wives may be a strengthening factor to some marriages but a detriment to others. Therefore, to simply advocate that working wives (and/or working mothers) is a personal matter, or suggest that it is a neutral subject, may be begging the question. Each couple must reckon with their own situation in light of social mores, the motivations for two wage earners, the effects upon family life and personal life-styles, and the effect upon their commitment to Christ. A smaller tithe or offering may be far superior if it frees parents from pressure and gives them more time together and time which can be shared with their children (or parents/grandparents, neighbors, and friends). When a recent study revealed that reasonably successful marriages involve a mere four minutes per day of communication between husband and wife (twenty-seven minutes per week), imagine what fifteen or thirty minutes per day of in-depth communication might accomplish. Communication between spouses is not optional.

If sexual intercourse is the most intimate form of communication known (few would deny this although in most marriages there is always room for improvement), fidelity must spill over into other aspects of wedded life. When spouses belittle each other, make subtle but hardly harmless digs at one another, especially in public, marriage is undermined. Dinner conversations need not be punctuated with private tales or suggestive barbs. There are matters so personal that no one should be initiated into these intimacies. Furthermore, few know a person better than a spouse, and this includes strengths and weaknesses, idiosyncrasies and habits, and a host of other human foibles.

Adultery is more than a sexual infidelity. It is anything which ultimately contributes to a lack of confidence or a breach of communication at its most intimate and deepest level.

Divorce, according to the Scriptures, is a complicated subject and needs more detailed consideration than there is space for here. However, at times couples either bail out too readily or hang in far longer than is healthy. Scripture sometimes is either interpreted or ignored so that it defends our position because of the sensitivity of the controversy involved. This commandment, although it speaks to the integrity and fidelity of those sharing their lives together, does make us aware of the awesome consequences of crumbling marriages as well as broken homes.

We would do well to make divorce, dissolution, and desertion separate matters but we tend to lump them together. The same would be true with the many causes of the malfunctioning of marriage including insensitivity, infidelity, irresponsibility, continence, promiscuity, brutality, addiction, and incompatibility. The breakdown of a marriage is often a complicated, emotionally-charged, frustrating matter.

Since the Bible makes it clear that a dehumanizing philosophy advocating *sexual intercourse for pleasure with consenting partners done with discretion* is not what the Creator had in mind, the One who created the sexual urge in the first place must have also created within humankind the capacity to manage without this form of gratification. Sexual urges we know are powerful with the young who are not seemingly ready for marriage (at least in our culture). To argue that marriage, if entered into early in life, is a satisfactory way of sublimating these urges, is to err. Singles, whether youth or adults, previously married or not, can by the grace of God manage without sexual intercourse as part of their life-style.

But, once having experienced this pleasure, abstention or prohibition is another matter. Knowing that the Creator has made us what we are, with powerful sex drives, any prohibition either of fornication or adultery must be also related to its aftermath. Many cry because of the loneliness caused by the empty half of a double bed. Statistics also indicate that many of these missing bed partners are replaced, one way or another. Seemingly this practice is also making significant inroads into the Christian community as well. Once having experienced the joys and intimacies of wedded life, the aches of a celibate life often become unbearable. Even the apostle Paul recognized this problem as he pointed out that it is better to marry than to be *aflame with passion* (1 Cor. 7:9).

The effect, so often negative, of broken marriages upon children, relatives, and friends is astounding. The waves caused by marital disorders range from ripples to tidal waves, but the converse is also true—stable, loving, positive marriages calm troubled waters. Although it is true that divorce or dissolution may at times be necessary—not only for a spouse but for children and other relatives involved—there is an inherent danger of rushing into separation as the optimum solution. It can be but is not necessarily so. When a society discovers itself caught up in a maze of broken families, there may be little or no hope for survival. An occasional marriage may go bad with a gentle mixing of spouses, stepchildren and grandparents; that society can handle. But when divorce becomes an epidemic, society cannot possibly cope with it for long. The human race just does not have the emotional capacity to handle the breakdown of marriage.

If marriage is so sacred, so significant, that one out of the ten moral principles of the universe is addressed to it, what about the alternatives to marriage?

These alternatives are legion but we'll limit ourselves to only a few. We have already hinted at what could be called the *tandem marriage*—a form of living together successively with one spouse after another. Multiple marriages of one or both spouses is too common, ending only when the marriage seems to be highly satisfying to both partners or one has an ingenious knack of keeping the marriage intact.

Another common practice is the *common law* arrangement. Often considered legally and otherwise as marriage, this is a mutually agreed-upon living relationship between two consenting adults whereby marriage vows and ceremonies are waived. Although studies reveal that many of these so-called marriages are quite successful, it might be added that in many of these successes, if not most, the basic ingredients of marriage are intact—fidelity, loyalty, mutual sharing love, understanding. Indeed, a marriage could exist apart from legal papers and ceremonies. In our society, however, necessary papers and legal procedures are essential for a variety of reasons.

There is another popular and rather widespread arrangement whereby two agree to live together. In some circles these are known as Living Together Arrangements (LTA). For reasons ranging from attraction and lust to economic convenience, couples agree to become roommates instead of husband and wife. In the typical LTA there is not the fidelity of common law, and partners are free, within reason, to come and go. This rather whimsical arrangement has been and will be tested in the courts with varying results. One would think that this kind of living together would be quite stable because of the necessity of clinging together without the support of legal papers or the blessings of significant segments of society. But studies show otherwise.

When homosexuals seek authorization to become legally married, marriage—at least in the biblical sense—is inappropriate. To be sure, many aspects of marriage could apply—togetherness, fidelity, affection, legal privileges, and even sexual gratification. This cannot and should not be classed as marriage. If there is to be any sanction given legally, and it appears that this may be the case, the term *marriage* is a misnomer.

When it comes to a biblical understanding of marriage, we are disturbed by the numerous instances of multiple spouses. Solomon, a flagrant polygamist, was used to exalt monogamous marriage. On the other hand, when Abraham took his handmaiden who later gave birth to his son Ishmael, this was not sanctioned. Whether God merely tolerated or approved polygamy is debatable. My personal opinion bends sharply in the direction of tolerance. To argue that if God wanted man to have more than one wife, He would have given Adam at least two is a moot question. Inferences from silence are not always admissable in court. Why God didn't more often visibly reprimand some of His stalwarts who made a habit of getting married repeatedly remains a mystery. King David, who resorted to murder by remote control in order to attain Bathsheba, was soundly denounced for his behavior. Even so, David was not advised to give up Bathsheba. Bathsheba, in my judgment (see *Couples in the Bible* for more on David and his wives), turned out to be a marvelous match for David and God seemingly held no grudges as she became part of the lineage of the Messiah.

Someone has wisely said that *the best thing a man can do for his children is to love their mother*. We have discussed the strategic importance of the family, and it is strategic. But in all fairness, it must be at least suggested that *strong couples make strong families* and strong families perpetuate themselves. A couple is the vehicle God created to erase loneliness and bring about togetherness. Children can come between parents but it is not necessary nor is it desirable. Love expands to meet its demands. A couple is the way God intended for little ones to be brought into a chilly, hostile environment. Every little child ought to be wrapped in swaddling clothes and snuggled by both parents. The warmth and love given by loving parents is designed to offset the shock of an uncaring, selfish, sinful society.

Furthermore, there is safety in numbers. No two think alike, and we all behave differently as we are endowed by our Creator with distinguishing features—temperaments, personalities, dispositions, strengths, abilities, gifts, and insights. Single parents can and often do a significant job of raising little ones, and many of us share a God-given responsibility to aid in the process as *adopted* missing spouses, parents and grandparents, uncles and aunts, cousins, nieces and nephews, neighbors and friends. If a woman has lost her husband through death or divorce, why can't we men take little Johnny under our masculine wing in wisdom, love and discretion? Even so, the ideal is still unsurpassed: a loving father and mother devoted to giving their children a flying start on life, feathering the nest without overprotecting the occupant, eventually and appropriately watching the little bird wing its own way. To find the appropriate balance of child support is best done with reciprocal parents who amazingly and marvelously complement each other in the process called marriage. God knew what He was doing.

But, we argue, if God knew that sexual relationships between His created human beings were so important, why didn't He tell us more about it? Why all the prohibitions? Don't fornicate, don't commit adultery, marry for eternity, train up a child in the way he should go, love your wives, be submissive to your husbands . . . . Why nothing about sexual relationships within marriage? Couldn't He have given us a chapter or two on this?

Although so much more could and should perhaps be said about this matter, we will briefly close the chapter on this note. God did say something important about sexual relationships within marriage. In fact, it is not only specific, it is explicit. The tragedy is that so few know anything about God's perspective on sex and even worse, those who do probably miss the point because it is couched in symbolic language.

God does move in mysterious ways. He chose a person, possibly one most unlikely in our judgment, to speak about the beauty and dignity of marital fidelity. Solomon, of all people, with his 1,000 wives and concubines, did write about his special love, and he wrote about her in such intimate terms that one is amazed. It is difficult to talk about sexual intimacies of marital life in anything except medical or vernacular terms; both leave much to be desired. Solomon, however, rose above both in penning his love song in poetical, symbolical terms. Consequently, much of what he has said has been overlooked.

Solomon was initially Israel's richest, most impressive king. His love, as expressed so beautifully in the Song of Solomon, is a peasant girl. Talk about a potential incompatibility, an improbable match, an unrealistic situation. Here we have a sunburned peasant girl at work in a Lebanese field who attracts the attention of a traveling king. Solomon is stricken by her, but she knews this is a mismatch and resists his attempts to woo her. Solomon persists, however, and finally persuades her to marry him. They marry, take their honeymoon and life in the palace begins for Shulamite.

Whether Solomon wrote this memorable love song early in their marriage or later in life we have no way of knowing. My own feeling is that it reflects considerable wisdom as well as passion and probably was penned some time after he had been married to Shulamite. The Song of Solomon is a series of flashbacks on his relationship with his bride, beginning with preparations for the wedding and their wedding night. The details, writes Joseph H. Dillow in his fascinating study *Solomon on Sex* (which I urge you to read), "are erotically but tastefully described." The second half of the song deals with the agonies and ecstasies of the intimacies of wedded life. Dillow goes on, "She refuses his sexual advances one night, and the king departs. She, realizing her foolishness, gets up and tries to find him, eventually does, and they have a joyous time embracing again."

This love song is explicit although written in an Eastern symbolism. Therefore, Dillow does us a real favor in unravel-

ing the mysteries of the obscure Song of Solomon. You may or
may not agree with all his findings, but you will at least realize
that God, in His infinite wisdom, has not left us without divine
guidance on the intimacies of wedded life. The Song of Solomon is an amazing document, with insights only recently discovered, but without their limitations. God would not have us
ignorant and His enlightenment has been given, as always, on
the highest possible level.

When one realizes the infinite superiority of marital fidelity
and its accompanying bliss, is it any wonder that God condemned adultery?

FOR STUDY OR DISCUSSION

1. When we think of fidelity, music comes to mind. What is meant by high fidelity in marriage relationships?
2. Explain: "Without fidelity, marriage not only loses its luster, it loses its nature."
3. What is the difference between *fornication* and *adultery*? Why was the word *adultery* used?
4. Our culture and the ancient Hebrew culture have this in common: Sexual fidelity is surrounded by a sea of sexual freedom and infidelity. Does Scripture teach that sexual relationships outside of wedlock are not a part of God's "game plan"? Where is it written?
5. In what way does fidelity go beyond sex?
6. Is there any correlation between "stolen kisses" and the lack of a satisfying sexual relationship within marriage?
7. How does the unmarried spouse cope with single life after divorce, death, or desertion? Can God's grace cover loneliness and the willingness to forego sex?
8. Name some of the causes underlying a fading fidelity.
9. Define and illustrate "spiritual adultery." Is this similar to "emotional" or "psychological adultery"?
10. Examine this statement: "Anything which contributes directly or indirectly to the breakdown of marriage must be examined carefully." What are some of these "contributions"? What can be done about them?

Chapter Eight
GENEROSITY

You shall not steal
Exodus 20:15

It is more blessed to give
than to receive (Acts 20:35).

When the Israelites were trudging through the awesome
desert they couldn't accumulate very much in the way of
worldly goods. To pack and unpack, pack and repack, is no
fun. In fact, it might be advantageous to get ripped off.

We may wonder why there was a problem of stealing
among these nomadic people. There are a couple of clues.
Some 500 years before, Jacob fled from an unscrupulous
father-in-law. Before leaving, Rachel confiscated some of the
family heirlooms, small idols which she hid by sitting on them.
Therefore, they escaped detection when her father, Laban,
came searching. Evidently she considered the idols as we
would a good-luck charm and wanted them in her possession as
they made their journey.

Then when the Israelites thought Moses had died on the
Sinai mountain, Aaron asked for a collection of gold. From
every tent came a piece of gold—a trinket, possibly a goblet,
an earring, a brooch, maybe a coin. When Aaron melted these
valuables, he poured the gold into a mold, presumably life-
size. Imagine the amount of gold this would be and its enormous value, even then.

As the spiritual commitment of the Israelites waned, their family life disintegrated; as life itself became cheap, things took on more importance. Materialism always seems to be a symptom of an inner distress or insecurity. Generally, those who possess high self-esteem and positive values are not as tempted to acquire status or worldly goods as those with low esteem and disoriented value systems. Therefore, thievery began to haunt the twelve tribes until it warranted a commandment of its own.

Furthermore, the tenth command against coveting reveals another dimension of these tribal people. They were jealous of each other. When they left Egypt, they took with them favors from the Egyptians. Whether these were loans or gifts, tokens of love or sighs of relief, we can't be certain. But no doubt some families fared better than others; some probably flaunted their wealth or displayed their accumulations. Whatever, personal property lost its sacredness and stealing plagued them mercilessly. When we lose something of little value or sentiment, we shrug it off—but when we have taken from us an heirloom or an invaluable piece of merchandise, it not only terrorizes, it demoralizes. Accusations fly, retaliation broods and an ugly distrust sets in. Evidently an epidemic had hit these ancient people causing God's chisel to hit its target with no uncertainty: YOU SHALL NOT STEAL!

Some years ago, a popular national magazine told the story of "The Billion Dollar Scandal: They steal for the hell of it." This was an exposé of teenage shoplifting by youths from families with plenty of money—yet there were 15,000 shoplifting thefts per day. Now, as we reflect on this statistic we realize more than ever that when a practice becomes widespread it quickly becomes acceptable. Stealing, in all its blatant as well as subtle forms, is not only a monumental business, it is an assumed part of many cultures.

It is difficult to compete on a world scale because of the high incidence of absenteeism in the industrial world; it is difficult to cut taxes or keep them from soaring due to unreported income, graft, inefficiency and corruption; it is far from idealistic to graduate students who have plagiarized their way through school; it is difficult to develop sportsmanlike conduct when athletes are bribed to throw games or shave points; it is unedifying to see parishioners give pennies to Jesus while keeping the rest for themselves.

Too often we underestimate this commandment. When the Americana Hotel opened in New York City, it gave a ten-month operation report. There was a loss of 38,000 demitasse spoons, 18,000 towels, 335 silver coffee pots, 15,000 finger bowls, and would you believe—100 Bibles.

Stealing is a peculiar vice. We justify it as an absentminded quirk ("How'd that get into my suitcase?"). We steal because it's a form of entertainment, a dare, a challenge. The poor steal from the rich because they need, want, or believe they deserve it. The rich steal from the rich to give to the poor (Robin Hood). The rich steal from the poor because they can get away with it. The shrewd extort; the strong plunder; the weak black-mail; the knowledgeable misappropriate; punks pickpocket; terrorists hijack; opportunists poach; the sick are called klepto-maniacs and bankers embezzle.

Stealing is an act as well as a science. And, believe it or not, there are those who have no idea they are stealing. To them it is living by their wits. A fraud or a swindle is not wrong—it's a matter of wit, or skill. Some merely borrow with little or no intention of paying back. Others are freeloaders or leeches. Others exploit a system which might be legally right but mor-ally wrong. Since our English vocabulary is enormous—abduction, robbery, plagiarism, poaching, plundering, extor-tion, graft, burglary, pilfering, larceny and smuggling, to mention a few—the various shades of stealing are revealing. Stealing is not merely grand theft or petty shoplifting—steal-ing is one of God's comprehensive laws that cannot be broken. It instead breaks those who ignore or exploit it.

Stealing, in its original Hebrew form, comes from the root word which means to "thieve by deceiving." Literally, it means to carry away by stealth. Applying this to the context of its original audience, the ancient Hebrews, it would imply the act of sneaking into a neighbor's tent and taking something from it, hopefully without being seen or getting caught. This same process goes on today when Mom's purse is lightened by a sticky-fingered child or Dad's credit card is forged by an ingenious impostor or Grandpa is conned into taking money from his bank account never to see it or his "benefactor" again.

As with all of the commandments, we must begin with the most obvious meaning. Stealing moves from piggy bank pilfering to grand theft—and from shortchanging the cash register to rigging a computer. Stealing is not only taking something from someone, it is also depriving someone of a just due. In a sense God gambled on using the simple word *steal* because we often underestimate the magnitude of its scope.

APPLYING THE COMMAND

The whole economy of the world is summed up in this command. No matter what political or economic system we live under, this commandment is basic. It applied to the autonomous system enjoyed by Adam and Eve. They had the run of the garden with the exception of one tree which they were told not to touch or eat of its fruit. God had already imprinted on their hearts the impact of this eighth command: "Don't take anything that doesn't belong to you." They did, and we all know the result.

This same law applied to the ancient Hebrews who were told to keep out of their neighbor's tent. This command applied to the Romans who incurred the wrath of the Jews because of their ruthless exploitation. It applied to the church when Martin Luther was incensed at the strong-arm tactics of his fellow priests. In fact, this command never quits. It applies to all economic systems. It is inherent in all systems of collecting revenues ranging from tribute to taxes. When a government steals from its subjects or deprives them of their rights they are violating this eighth principle.

In this commandment we have the roots for the dignity of ownership, fiscal sanity, equitable wages and adequate incentives. Whenever a system encourages an irresponsible welfarism and indolence, something vital is lost. Even the complex intricacies of deficit spending weigh heavily on the conscience of this commandment. To "go now and pay later" has some built-in advantages but when exploited has enormous repercussions. It is unthinkable that a nation live beyond its means by placing an irresponsible financial burden on unborn generations. A deliberate inflation designed to push taxpayers into higher brackets may be just as much a violation of this principle as usury (the lending of money at an exorbitant rate of interest). Nations or individuals soon discover the ingenious wisdom in these four words: YOU SHALL NOT STEAL.

There is no way God could have chiseled a detailed divine economic blueprint into the rock Moses carried down the mountain, but He did the next best. He gave us a divine economic principle equally suitable for a godless communism or a wayward capitalism or any other system, benevolent or otherwise.

WHAT IS "STEALING"?

In order to establish some ground rules for family living, it may be well to spell some of the details in an alphabetical form. Any good thesaurus will show the magnitude of the synonyms for stealing. Not only will these expressions reveal the wide scope of the subject, they will give parents, teachers, pastors, and others a handle with which to deal biblically with the subject. If we are consciously aware of these wrongs, subtle and blatant, we can impress the next generation with the necessary sensitivity to deal with every sort of stealing—a process that must go on from sunup to sundown.

AVARICE is greed for material things. Its kinship to stealing is its capacity to rob children of a better heritage. Materialism is not the best foundation to lay for the better life. Indeed, the best in life may not be free, but the gnawing desire to acquire, achieve, and accelerate matters of comfort and prestige is too much a part of our culture to be overlooked by this eighth commandment.

BELITTLEMENT also stares at the family from every mirror. Husbands and wives too often flail each other with snide little digs or open hostility. Parents run their children down and then wonder why they fail to develop strong egos and wholesome self-esteems. Parents also, at times, consciously or unconsciously, belittle those who could do their children so much good—teacher, pastor, governor, president, coach, grandparent, bus driver (some get an hour or two a day with our children) and innumerable others. If we as adults belittle we can be quite assured that the next generation will be the losers.

BOREDOM is another form of theft. It is true that much in life must be boring but it is equally true that when all is boredom, something vital is taken from life. When parents are willing to make life interesting by sharing talents, skill, time, and interests with their children, keeping an eye open for the unusual, explaining caterpillars and bees, sonic booms and lightning, and planning some child-centered vacations and watching the best of TV together, we are not depriving them of their due.

A so-called CASTE SYSTEM does function in our society. We steal from one another by living in cliques and snubbing those who talk with an accent or laugh at the wrong times. It is easy to create a holier-than-you-are world. We dare not add to ourselves by taking from others.

CHEATING has become nearly as acceptable as shoplifting although both are wrong. Teachers cheat by being too lenient; students cheat by plagiarizing. Drivers cheat with a heavy foot, and taxpayers "forget" certain sources of income. At home is where we are most effective in curbing potential dishonest maneuvering, petty theft, "innocent" fraud and the bending of circumstances. Cheating, as a way of life, robs the soul as it empties the till.

DEPRIVATION is an unbelievable malady, perhaps second to its converse, indulgence (in an affluent society). Simply put, deprivation is withholding a right, not necessarily a privilege (although it can be that). Too often we want Johnny to be a sports hero and Suzy a famous violinist when Johnny actually should play the fiddle and Suzy should be a tennis whiz. To impose our will, noble as it is, can steal from our kin.

We not only impose our will (watch the relatives at a Little League game) but we are too often insensitive to the interests and aptitudes of our children. We do this in two ways: we are either too busy or we are not deeply enough involved. Parents would be wise to peek over the shoulders of their children when they do their homework. A good rapport should be established early in life so that our children will confide readily (unless established early, this easily degenerates into snooping). We deprive by giving too much too readily just as we deprive by robbing their piggy banks. Uncle Sam realized that some parents wouldn't get their kids off in the morning and made school mandatory. The same is true of Sunday School and optional piano lessons. A hand need not be turned into an iron fist but it should be strong.

EXPLOITATION isn't a pleasant word nor is it an honorable profession. Taking advantage of someone or something unfairly or even fairly but questionably, perhaps, is dangerous. At times it cannot be avoided (as parents who arm their children with "exploit" money when they go to school). This is sad. Many years ago some of the children in my parish often paid off their adversaries with their lunch money and never went into the school lavatories (they came to our church instead). How did we get into this sad state? It came about slowly as this commandment was shrugged off by well-meaning people.

With the problem increasingly displayed, GAMBLING needs a sharp word or two. There is of course a difference between flipping a coin to see who gets on the bus first and being a bookie. But bookies and casino operators seldom started under the auspices of a syndicate. Gambling, unfortunately, has a lot going for it—it's fun, exciting, challenging, and can be tremendously rewarding. It also has many legitimate supporters and is used in the form of lotteries or "lucky winners" by reputable enterprises. Most of us like to get something for nothing and we are an insatiable people in tracking down bargains. Besides, petty gambling in the minds of many is merely innocent fun.

Unfortunately, Gamblers Anonymous had to come into existence because gambling for many became compulsive and disruptive. Gambling is a form of cheating that thrives on exploiting one of the weaknesses of human nature.

GLUTTONY is unbiblical in that *man shall not live by bread alone*. Seriously, eating habits are formed very early in life. Overeating is one of the human predicaments in affluent times and becomes a sop when things aren't going too well. To be gluttonous is one thing; to pass it on to the next generation is another. We are told that overfeeding an infant, even though he or she seemingly demands it, can lead to a roly-poly existence in later life. Overindulgence of any kind is another form of stealing as it robs one of self-control as well as being unnecessarily expensive.

HUMANISM may not be thought of as stealing, and for a non-Christian it may not be (at least in the same sense). In short, humanism is an expansion of human virtues at the expense of the supernatural. God and divine matters are crowded out as the world around squeezes into its mold. To exclude biblical principles and spiritual dimensions from day-to-day living is regrettable.

Entertainment, mass media, peer pressure, the proliferation of school and community affairs (many of which are excellent) all tend to encourage a secular existence. God, and the church, may not be shunned, but their relevance is diminished and eventually can be virtually nil.

LAZINESS also robs. We all have a lazy bone somewhere. Children learn to procrastinate early in life. Whining, pouting, and tantrums may never be outgrown. The development of self-discipline, promptness and trustworthiness are not automatic and our methods of handling indolence and self-discipline can be counterproductive, too.

MISERLINESS is an ugly malady. It is one thing to be a spendthrift; it is quite another to be stingy. Both blight the human soul. Hoarding can be a lesson in doubting and frugality can be a virtue. My childhood was spent crawling through the Depression. Fortunately, my memory is rather dim and my pre-teenage years were not very perceptive economically. I do remember, however, being the only kid in school wearing knickers. For some reason they refused to wear out, and as long as they were wearable I had to wear them. But they did help the family budget though they did nothing for my self-esteem. Savings at any cost may be too high a price. What goes on at home is important—from tithing to piggy banks, from attitudes of generosity to miserliness, from extravagance to shoddiness.

PETTY THEFT or pilfering is where it begins. When little ones are taught that fibbing and helping themselves to things that do not belong to them is wrong, it will be more difficult later to justify inappropriate behavior. It's amazing how "little white lies" can evolve into "harmless" deception and petty theft can grow into grand larceny. The moral of the story: "Don't underestimate the long-lasting impressions made in the home, especially the downplay of potentially explosive matters such as pilfering, petty thievery and plagiarism. The amount of cheating in the schoolroom (on all levels) and stealing in the marketplace (short workdays, long lunch breaks, personal use of company telephones and supplies) is staggering.

RETALIATION deserves a line or two in this stealing glossary. When we are victimized by either petty thievery or a major burglary, it is natural to want restitution or revenge. At times this is impossible; sometimes the urge for revenge lasts a lifetime, affecting not only the avenger but family and friends. Retaliation usually isn't worth the effort but it does reveal another negative effect of stealing. *Restitution*, an art of fading value, is important biblically. To repay someone is not always considered necessary, and when it is it is often done grudgingly. These two *R*s are important precepts to be taught at home: *retaliation* blights the soul but *restitution* can be a blessing beyond measure.

USURY, as we have noticed, generally means lending at an excessive rate of interest. At the time these commandments were written, the Hebrews were not allowed to lend to one another. But that should be clarified. If taxes (or tribute) were due, for instance, and a farmer hadn't harvested and sold his crop, he could get an advance from a fellow herdsman who had sold some sheep. In exchange for this loan, a form of security was necessary. This security was returned when the loan was repaid. Therefore, no interest was involved. However, if there had been a crop failure, and the security was kept, a form of usury had taken place. Besides human nature being what it is, all kinds of economic mischief was possible.

The lending and borrowing of money between relatives and friends has an astonishingly poor track record. When members of the same congregation borrow and lend in good faith and repayment is not made, the whole body suffers. The same is true in the family. Therefore, we must take considerable care as we instruct the incoming generation on the economic facts of life relative to lending and repaying—from a boy who lends his catcher's mitt to his brother who loses it, to loan sharks who eat people alive. As with all illustrative measures, the spirit of the law supercedes the letter. Therefore, even though *retaliation* and *usury* can be negative factors, the underlying principle is more important than we may think.

WINNING AT ANY COST is losing. We can steal all the joy from games and sports and from those who play them with very little effort. Winning is important, but it's far better to steal second base and get caught than to steal the integrity of a Little Leaguer who feels he must win regardless. When win, win, win is pumped into open minds they soon become closed. Try this quiz with the Little League system and with your church athletes:

Yes Maybe No

1. ___ ___ ___ Our main objective is to win.

2. ___ ___ ___ Our main objective is to play the best game possible whether we win or lose.

3. ___ ___ ___ We spend a great share of our time dealing with the art of team play and sportsmanship and gentlemanly conduct, on

and off the playing field (court).

4. ___ _____ ___ We sulk when our team loses.

5. ___ _____ ___ We praise a better team (or an excellent player) openly.

6. ___ _____ ___ We discipline a player who displays unsportsmanlike conduct (or disobeys the rules, coach, referee, etc.).

7. ___ _____ ___ We point to outstanding athletes who are great examples of the virtues we are stressing (and vice versa).

8. ___ _____ ___ In our church team, we play only the best players unless we are way ahead or far behind.

9. ___ _____ ___ We remind our players that natural and developed athletic abilities are God-given attributes.

10. ___ _____ ___ In our church team, we use sports to interest, hold, and strive to win persons for Christ and His kingdom.

The above quiz is self-revealing. For Christians, at home and in the church, athletics can be used to enrich or impoverish.

THE OPPOSITE OF STEALING

A veteran physician once said that he never knew a truly generous person who ever had a nervous breakdown. Expanding on this, psychiatric wards would be empty if they depended only on selfless, generous people. This does not mean that generous people have no problems; it does mean that generosity has some invaluable fringe benefits.

Let's amplify this a little. If stealing is taking away, the opposite is giving. It is possible to give generously but reluctantly. We remember the wife who asked her husband for a little spending money. His reply highlights the problem, "Sure, honey, how little?" We've been told to give until it hurts. Ouch! That's not nearly as appropriate as giving until it feels good.

Generosity is not giving recklessly. Spenders are not necessarily generous. Many give to be seen, to impress, to manipulate. Parents give freely to get children from underfoot: "Go to a movie." "Take your junior year abroad." We smile at the parent who sent his son to college, then shrugged, saying, "I spent $35,000 on the kid and all I got was a quarterback." Are we generous in picking up the tab when our motives are ulterior? Hardly.

Generosity is more than spending. It's an attitude more than an act. It is "nobleness or liberality of nature: magnanimity or munificence in an act or acts" (*Chambers Everyday Dictionary*, Edinburg, 1975). Its root (*généreux* in French, *generosus* Latin), of noble birth, is more than birth (*genus*). Nobility suggests high rank, excellence, greatness of mind or character; it also means a person of exalted rank. Magnanimity suggests greatness of soul, a quality that raises a person above all that is unjust and mean; and munificence is another word for bountifulness—liberality in giving.

When a burglar enters our home, we hardly lecture him on the better way of living. Rather, we scream, "You shall not steal!" Had the good Lord more time and stone on Sinai, He might have also chiseled the converse: *It is more blessed to give than to take*. But the Israelites were robbing each other, plundering ruthlessly, burglarizing tents, and God was blunt: If it's not yours, leave it alone!

Still, God is magnanimous. Generosity, as a life-style, is supreme. Sharing our lives with those we love, sharing our means with those who need, brings a nobility to our lives. Strange, but among the earliest words a child learns are the revealing phrases, "Mine" and "*Gimme* dat." Human nature is not naturally generous. If we want to enrich the lives of those entrusted to us as well as our own, we will teach not only that stealing is bad but that generosity is good.

FOR STUDY OR DISCUSSION

1. Stealing cuts an enormous swath through life. Make a list of *tangibles* and *intangibles* that can be subject to

theft.

2. What are some of the ways stealing is "justified" in our society? What is wrong with this reasoning?

3. What is meant by the expression: "In a sense God gambled on using the simple word *steal*"?

4. What is the relationship of this command to a world economic or political system? How can socialism be guilty, how can communism be guilty, how can capitalism be guilty of violating the spirit of this axiom: *you shall not steal*?

5. What is meant by the "dignity of ownership"?

6. How can we teach our children that stealing is wrong, injurious, unfair, tempting, sinful, easy, daring, widespread, etc.?

7. Benevolent thievery (Robin Hood style) is a common practice and at times seemingly justifiable. Where have you experienced this? How would you explain its wrongfulness?

8. Is there anything wrong with exploiting a weakness of human nature (e.g. gambling—taking chances, lotteries, sweepstakes, flipping coins, etc.)? What is the difference between *exploiting* and *participating*? Does this commandment address both?

9. What are some of the more subtle forms of stealing?

10. How can we steal against God?

Chapter Nine

VERACITY

You shall not bear false witness
Exodus 20:16

Blessed are the pure in heart,
for they shall see God (Matt.
5:8).

When an Israelite was caught with a neighbor's precious heirloom hidden in his tent, what would he do? He'd probably do the same as thieves do today: "I have no idea how that got there"; "I was just playing a practical joke on you"; "You know me, I'd never do anything like that"; "I think someone stole it and planted it in my tent to make it look as though I did it."

Later, when this Israelite stood accused before Moses, he was in double jeopardy. Few of his friends would testify in his favor. He had been a good neighbor. He had never stolen before. He was a good husband and good father, but no one would say so. He stood condemned by silence, a form of bearing false witness. Another who did testify remembered one incident in the defendant's youth and prejudiced Moses with his hardly relevant evidence. Another, infamous for his indiscretions, who barely knew the defendant, lied about his character. Moses, fortunately for the defendant, was able to separate fact from fiction, truth from half-truths, and executed an equitable judgment.

The long lines appearing before Moses and his appointed justices hint at the degenerative character of the people. Lying, false accusations, and gossip plagued the wanderers on their way to the Promised Land. When people lose their sensitivity toward God and people, commit adultery and steal, bearing false witness is inevitable.

This commandment can be shattered by telling the truth.

We have been able to rationalize the consequences of the sixth through the eighth commandments because we tend to feel that these are aimed at notorious sinners (killers, adulterers, thieves). This ninth commandment, however, comes pretty close to home.

Lying is common to every family. Somehow it comes too easily and too early in life. A very young child will lie, fib, or sidestep the truth if he feels that it is to his advantage. And often it is—at the moment, perhaps. In all fairness, this commandment goes far beyond lying although it does cry out against it. In some ways, this commandment is one of the most crucial principles of the entire second half of the Decalogue. The previous three are aimed at the person himself and his property; this principle is aimed at his reputation—his name. It is no wonder that the Lord told us to love our neighbors as we love ourselves. This is not easy, and once again we are reminded that it is impossible in our own strength. The Ten Commandments do dramatically reveal our shortcomings.

Veracity is more abstract, somewhat more difficult to deal with than some of the other commandments. Veracity is more than truthfulness; it involves the whole dimension of character. A veracious person is known by his lack of guile, his passion to be truthful; he is also known for his reliability, precision, and accuracy. He does not repeat tidbits of gossip or make glib generalizations. He gives the benefit of a doubt, but calls 'em as he sees 'em. He goes one step further and refuses to speak even the truth if he suspects that it will do *unwarranted* damage to the reputation of the person involved. He does not engage in speaking half-truths. Veracity involves more than the tongue; it is concerned with the motives behind the utterance as well as possible consequences.

WHAT IS UNTRUTH?

Beginning with some of the negative dimensions, let's examine some of the practical ways in which we as parents and children alike violate this commandment. Since this commandment is concerned with interpersonal relations (family affairs, neighbor relations, employer-employee, and countless other personal relationships), each of us is involved more than we realize.

Outright lying is condemned. Once a person has been known to lie with deliberation, something suffers in a personal relationship. When a parent lies to a child knowingly and intentionally, there is trouble just around the corner. When a child fibs, or tells a "little white lie" (whatever that might be), or lies outright, the parent has an opportunity to zero in before it gets out of hand. Lying can become a way of life, a disease, a contagion leading eventually to chronic lying.

We have been admonished legally to "tell the truth, the whole truth, and nothing but the truth." *Half-truths* can be deliberate ways of obscuring what actually occurred or they can be innocent misrepresentations. The motive behind a half-truth is critical.

Blessed is the person in whom there is no *guile*. Deliberately creating a misleading impression by telling the whole truth or a half-truth is bearing false witness. A person can tell the truth and nothing but the truth and create an erroneous impression. The tone of voice, the audience, the setting, the mood—all of these must be considered. A potential blind date could be pegged as bowlegged, plump, poverty-stricken with a bad case of halitosis. Who then would want to date her? Furthermore, it could be true. But it might be that she is less than wealthy, slightly but barely noticeably bowlegged, pleasingly plump and in need of mouthwash after a long hard day in the office. It could also have been pointed out that she has a radiant personality and is the life of the party. The ninth commandment is death on guile!

Hypocrisy follows on the heels of guile. Not enough can be said about living honestly, admitting shortcomings, punctuating vocabularies with "I'm sorry" and living consistent lives on both Sunday and Monday. We are told not to bear false witness which includes both what we say and what we do. We have no right to not "practice what we preach." Children have sensitive *antennae*, and with their perceptive radar, most siblings can detect phonies with little difficulty. Adults can fool adults much of the time, but children are not fooled so easily.

This principle also is concerned with *gossip*. Gossip can be harmless (chatting idly about others), although it usually isn't. Probing more deeply into a reported definition of gossip, there is the added dimension of spreading rumors about the private or personal life of others. Again, gossip may be the truth based on fact but violates this ninth commandment in that it creates a misleading impression. We all struggle with this malady. Gossip is often small talk, often malicious and damaging to the reputation. Even when gossip is proven wrong, the mere planting of a rumor is damaging. Reversing harm done by gossip is difficult if not impossible. Explanations and apologies are at best difficult and usually do not occur. Therefore, the commandment stands: Idle talk, gossip, rumor, palaver and hearsay all violate the spirit of this declaration.

Slander is a deliberate attempt to injure another individual. In a sense it violates the command in two ways. Again it may be true, even horribly true, but when it is used to deliberately damage the reputation of a person rather than execute justice (as in a trial or hearing), it violates this commandment. We do not have the right to tell the truth (or a falsehood) which will maliciously harm another. Slander is a statement, made or implied, designed to injure the reputation of the intended victim. Slander becomes calumny when it is rumor loaded with deception. The tragedy of slander is that it is often so subtle, so ingenious, and so effective.

In fact, sometimes we go to the other extreme. We avoid possible slander and become innocuous, imperceptive and unreliable in our judgment of others. We see this in confidential reports made on prospective students or employees. Often the one who makes a recommendation avoids defaming an individ-

ual by withholding valuable information. Glossing over negative attributes or going too far in "giving the benefit of a doubt"
is another way in which this ninth command is broken.

During election time we listen to a lot of campaign oratory
which is often loaded with *glib promises or idle threats*. This is
also a sin found in courtship: "If you marry me I'll give you
half of my kingdom" (even though the poor bloke doesn't even
own a bicycle). In all fairness, there are a lot of campaign oratory and courtship promises which are highly seasoned with
more hope than guile. Exaggeration can be a form of false witness although it need not be.

Parents are great offenders in making *idle threats*. Children
will be threatened, for instance, with an allowance curtailment,
but it doesn't occur. After a while the youngster realizes that
this is mere rhetoric. Threats, if made, should be carried out or
they shouldn't be made in the first place.

Most of us like to hear our name, and we enjoy a compliment even more. At times we'll break this ninth commandment
in order to realize our fondest wishes. One way to feel taller is
to make another appear shorter. We can minimize the strengths
of others to maximize our own; we often climb over others to
get to the top. These are subtle ways of bearing false witness,
and some are guilty of doing this sort of thing most inge-
niously. Furthermore, a reputation can be damaged by the
slightest flick of an eyebrow, a carefully planted hint, a strate-
gically placed utterance, a backhanded compliment. One of the
most amazing words of all is that three letter word b-u-t. She is
a gifted musician *but* . . . He is one of the greatest surgeons in
America *but* . . . She had a fine report card *but* . . . The
inability to give credit to whom credit is due (or to tone it
down) is also a violation of this ninth maxim.

In the courtroom *perjury* plays a significant role. Telling a
falsehood while under oath is condemned by the Decalogue
and democracy alike. No civilized society can survive unless
truth reigns. Today it seems that we have bent over too far in
protecting the guilty by over-encouraging the use of the Fifth
Amendment (*I refuse to answer on the grounds that it might*

tend to incriminate me). This is a necessary safeguard to human rights and to the judicial system, but when it is abused it becomes a violation of the ninth command. It is a violation in that it creates a wrong impression, implicates the innocent, or frustrates justice. Justice cannot occur when a guilty party goes free simply because no one will testify, or when perjury is committed. Justice is seeing that truth prevails—is at the heart of the ninth commandment.

Blackmail also is a violation of the ninth precept. It is a dastardly deed. Girls, for example, can be lured into prostitution through blackmail, and these same girls often choose to remain rather than run the risk of having the "truth" told. In many cases involving blackmail, truth is used to intimidate. Extortion, blackmail, slander, and perjury are all intricately interwoven—one begins where another ends—and life lived in this manner is a tragedy.

We find subtle forms of false witness occurring regularly in the home: "Oooooooh, I've got a vicious headache; I can't go to church today." This is bearing false witness when the headache is existent but hardly disabling. Parents are conned regularly and so are children: "If you don't clean your room, Mommie won't love you any more." What a way to bear false witness! Husbands and wives can con each other, and often with extreme finesse. Some spouses become masters at blackmail. Children victimized by broken homes often learn to manipulate, usually at the expense of one of the parents if not both.

During a quarrel the wife broke a vase over her husband's head making an ugly gash requiring fourteen stitches. Said she, "If you'll say that you fell down the stairs I won't go to court." He, wanting to patch things up, said that he'd simply say he had an accident. She, a stubborn, jealous woman, haughty and proud, broke the ninth by telling their daughters that their clumsy father injured himself through his own stupidity. Bearing false witness can become awfully involved, and it can be a most insidious form of evil. No wonder an entire commandment was given to it.

WHAT IS TRUTH?

The flip side of this record has a melody played in a major key—and what a monumental piece of music it is. Let's take a look at the kind of life we can and ought to live as parents (and children) when we take the ninth command seriously.

In some cultures it is not uncommon for people to commit suicide when they have lost face; in most cultures, many commit psychological suicide when they are victimized in this way. By digging deeply into the wording of this command—*You shall not bear false witness *against* your neighbor*—we find its most profound meaning. Simply changing it to read in the positive sense misses the point, not entirely, but significantly—Be truthful in your relationships with your neighbor. As we have pointed out, in some instances it is better not to say anything. The truth can be unnecessary. This command goes far beyond lying and telling the truth. It involves not only one's reputation, it also has some fringe benefits.

Someone wisely said that when you tell the truth you never have to remember what you've said. Guesswork is terribly hazardous, not only in the initial guess but in remembering how you guessed. When a lie (or half-truth) is told, the speaker must remember what he said, to whom, where, and when. What a burden to place on the human psyche. Parents must remember this when dealing with children. Never should a parent deliberately tell a falsehood to a child. The child may never get over the hurt. When we don't know something, we do the child a favor by telling him we don't know (depending of course on how we tell him).

When I was in college, a professor went to great lengths to argue that a lie is never justifiable. I was convinced at the time that he was right. Since then I've had some doubts. I could think of innumerable instances when a lie (deliberate deception) would not only be practical but honorable. For instance, telling an armed, enraged, drunken husband that his wife ran out the back door when in fact she was hiding behind the sofa could save her life. I could also envision being on a military mission and, because of a shrewd deception, was able to save a battalion of soldiers. Do the words of the command "against thy neighbor" make bearing false witness unjustifiable unless it helps our neighbor? Bearing false witness against someone seems to suggest that we have an obligation to protect life and reputation but we have no right to manipulate the truth without just cause. Even then we must remember that bearing false witness can involve unusual extenuating circumstances. This is the way we must live with our neighbor whom we must love as we love ourselves. Our neighbor's reputation and character is our concern.

For a Christian to be engaged in espionage, to work for one's country against an enemy and not employ deception or subterfuge is unthinkable. For some it is possible but the conscience of another would not allow it. Even in this kind of situation, does the end justify the means? If protecting our neighbor, his life, and his reputation can only be done by subterfuge, could the end justify the means? To cry to an enraged husband "She went that way" when in fact she didn't, indicates that common sense must be coupled intricately to motives. For some Christians it would appear to be best to avoid working for the CIA just as for others it is best not to bear arms or join the police corps.

We should also remind ourselves that we may be forced at times into breaking one command to save another. An officer may lie to save his troops; a starving man may resort to stealing to feed his family. The issuance of the Ten Commandments must not militate against the use of reason and common sense. God created the human race with intelligence and intended that we exercise sound judgment based upon the lasting principles which He gave. Therefore, the understanding and application of one law is often greatly dependent upon the knowledge and understanding of another. Our ethical decisions *must* be based upon eternal principles, not on societal mores or personal whimsy, even when we are forced into difficult, conflicting situations.

Self-esteem is one of the most important aspects of the

human personality. We talk a lot about the ego and what happens when it is overly weak or too strong. The person who needlessly maligns another, who spreads malicious gossip or uses another person to elevate himself cannot possibly have very high self-esteem. He may have a tough ego, and his psyche may be virtually indestructible (no mental breakdowns for him—he'll break someone else down first), but he won't have a wholesome self-esteem. He won't be able to carry his head very high and his heart will be empty. It's amazing, and I suppose we don't think a great deal about it, but no one except the One who designed us fully knows the emptiness of a human soul which appears to have much but in truth has little going for him. Living without guile, with malice toward none, with no psychological hangups because of a hatred for a brother or resentment caused by maliciousness, does not go unnoticed or unrewarded. A person can have nothing of this world's goods, but if he lives without guile, he has a wealth not understood by the slanderer, the perjurer, or the reputation pirate. Observing this ninth principle puts something into the heart of man which is worth far more than gold.

There is something honorable about those who refuse to bear false witness against a neighbor, friend, or relative. This is a principle which does wonders in winning friends and influencing people. We appreciate those who are truly interested in others rather than in themselves, who are concerned about their neighbors, who will listen sympathetically and volunteer assistance without a condescending attitude. The person who has no desire to harm soon wins the friendship and confidence of his neighbor. Everyone needs a confidant (a person to whom we confide secrets or with whom we have in-depth discussions of a personal and intimate nature). A person to whom we can go, knowing that our confidence will not be betrayed, is a blessing everyone needs. These are rare individuals, but what satisfaction there is in sharing someone else's burden.

We live in a day when sensitivity training is not only popular but to a degree necessary. Up to a certain point, sensitivity can be taught, and people can train and be trained in sensitivity.

It can also become a fad—the "in" thing to do. This is achieved in a variety of ways, from psychological undressing to exercises in listening. The Lord seemed to anticipate the hardening of human sensitivities when he issued the "blueprint" we are now studying. The sixth step addressed itself to the need to treat every human being, regardless of race, color, or creed, with sensitivity; the seventh step touched on the sensitivity necessary in intimate marital relationships. The eighth step stressed the dignity of ownership and sensitivity toward personal belongings. Now we find that our neighbor is terribly important, so important that we dare not injure his reputation, his name, his honor; in fact, we are suggesting that we go one step further and help him to better himself, to love him as we love ourselves, to share our insights, our hopes and dreams, our faith and our disciplines with him. The individual who reverses this command is not only sensitive to his neighbor, he becomes indignant when he sees his neighbor suffer an injustice, when someone maligns him, frustrating him from becoming what he ought to become and wants to become in the sight of Almighty God. The believer, the loving parent who, for the sake of his fellowman or a child, has never felt the pangs of *righteous indignation* is missing a great blessing.

A godly father cannot sit idly by and watch others tamper with the self-esteem and reputation of his family. A mother should get angry when she sees people bargain for the souls of her children; a child of God will not be at peace until hucksters who trade sons and daughters for a mess of pottage are eliminated. This kind of anger does not result in mental breakdowns; to the contrary, it lets adults sleep in peace when the curtain of night falls.

When God ordered the human race to refrain from bearing false witness, He had the twentieth century in mind as well as the fifth or tenth, both B.C. and A.D. Every day we are bombarded with a legion of insinuations, half-truths, outright lies, deception and evasive, hollow persuasions that bear false witness. Blessed are they who stand against false witnesses. No one can take the ninth commandment seriously and live a colorless, bland, innocuous life.

Horizons will be broadened; color blindness will fade. Concern over both the native in Zaire and the blighted soul in Harlem will mount. Harmful effects of air pollution, narcotic addiction, insurance abuses, crippling strikes affecting innocent victims will disturb the conscience. Life will be anything but dull; one may suffer from fatigue but never from boredom.

Ironically, we will also become better students of Scripture. We dare not allow a church (or a minister) to dispense trivia or false doctrine. We will become watchdogs lest false witnesses deceive. This could well be the most blatant form of violation of this commandment—men of God making cheap talk. If we cannot believe our minister (or priest), whom can we believe? Frankly, many men of the cloth have lost their way—so have churches for that matter. One of the greatest blessings of this commandment is not found in those who become heresy hunters (the spirit of this utterance forbids this low form of sniping) but in those who defy false witness as they rejoice in the truth. As it is more blessed to give than to receive, it is more blessed to give a man the truth than merely keep falsehood from him. The person who observes this command to its fullest is the most blessed.

Jesus summed it up beautifully when He said *Blessed are the pure in heart, for they shall see God*. He also said blessed are the *peacemakers*, and blessed are those who shall be *persecuted* for righteousness' sake—for theirs is the kingdom of God. Nothing on earth compares to purity in heart, the soul without guile, the heart which knows no deceit. And when holy people and godly parents lose their sense of direction, we can take heart in that there is no authority higher or more reliable than God's holy Word, of which the Decalogue is a most significant part.

FOR STUDY OR DISCUSSION

1. How can we bear false witness by telling the truth?
2. If we kill, commit adultery, and steal, is it logical to lie about it? Discuss the logic of the order of the command-

ments (particularly six-nine).

3. Although murder, infidelity, and stealing are sins of murderers, adulterers, and thieves, this command has a different intent. It is designed to protect a person's reputation. Does this mean it should be handled differently? If so, how?

4. How important is a wholesome self-love in God's scheme? Key: Love your neighbor *as* you love yourself (in the same manner or at the same time?). Why do we get caught on the two extremes—self-love (as conceit) versus self-deprecation (as worthlessness)?

5. Is a lie ever justifiable? For instance, *If he ever lies to me I'll never trust him again* versus *If he ever tells the truth I'll never trust* (confide in) *him again*. How do we reconcile these difficulties?

6. If the spirit of the command is to protect the integrity of a person or situation, is there ever any justification of half-truths, fibs, evasions, or other tactical maneuvers? If so, when?

7. How can gossip violate this command? Are there degrees or kinds of gossip?

8. How can we violate this command other than by words? How vulnerable is a single parent (e.g. casting an ex-spouse in an erroneous light)?

9. What is the real motive behind this command?

10. What responsibility do we have toward the reputation of others (children, parents, neighbors, friends, enemies, our spouse)?

Chapter Ten

SERENITY

You shall not covet
Exodus 20:17

> Blessed are those who
> hunger and thirst for
> righteousness, for they shall
> be satisfied (Matt. 5:6).

The ancient Israelites were human. In fact, we might say, too human. They embodied every grace and vice of humanity as they are depicted as a prototype of every nation. To say that Scripture singled out the Hebrews of yesterday to embarrass the Jews of today is unwarranted. The God of Abraham and Moses is the God of Calvin and Luther, King James and Queen Esther. However, in limiting the involvement of God's action in human history, all other nations are incidental, although not insignificant. To know and understand the twelve tribes of Israel is to know humanity at its best and at its worst.

Just as the laws of gravity and the invention of the wheel are inviolate, so are the moral laws of creation. They can be ignored, bent out of shape, or stretched beyond recognition, but they remain the same—eternal. Even so, seemingly each generation must experience the frustrations which accompany the disregarding of these laws as well as the rewards of following them.

The Exodus generation of Israelites had spent forty years in the wilderness, testing, ignoring, violating, and obeying the Decalogue. They had told the God of their fathers that they could do quite well without Him. They tried to skip the Sabbath, making every day alike. They neglected to impress upon their children the necessity of honoring parenthood. They slipped into their neighbor's tent to steal an heirloom and then lied about it. They slept with their neighbor and wondered where the sanctity of marriage went. They became jealous of the achievements of their more industrious tribesmen and coveted their cattle and servants alike. When all else failed, or when tempers went berserk, they murdered.

That's the negative side of the horror story of mankind. But there is also the positive side. The Israelites—and undoubtedly there were some—who kept the Ten Commandments, who loved their God as well as their neighbor, were rewarded. This reward is internal, not necessarily external, and comes in the glorious fashion of serenity—an inner peace that passes all understanding. That is the essence of this final commandment, it is also the reward which accompanies the keeping of the law.

Which would you rather have: twenty children or a million dollars?

When asked this question, a woman promptly replied, "Twenty children." Her reasoning? If she had twenty children, she would have enough; if she had a million dollars, she would want more.

We smile, don't we? But she is probably right. Most of us with twenty children would be satisfied, but with wealth we might never find contentment.

Not unlike the other commandments, this last utterance has the dimension of *universality*—it speaks about a malady of humankind in times of plenty and in times of want. It also has the dimension of *finality*.

IN TIMES OF WANT

In times of want we often crave what someone else has; in times of plenty we are impoverished by the inability to be satisfied with what we have. Both of these vices are violations of this last command.

Hovering over both of these extremities is an awful appetite called *greed*. Greed comes in all colors and sizes and is no respecter of persons. The wise apostle said once that "the love of money is the root of all evil." Some reactors argue that he meant "all sorts of evil"; others believe that Paul meant that the love of money was "a" not "the" root of evil; and many mistakenly have quoted Paul as saying that "money is the root of all evil." Looking back to the initiation of sin in the Garden of Eden, it could be said that Adam and Eve's greed was the major temptation in their act of disobedience which plunged the human race into darkness. No matter how we look at it, greed is behind an enormous amount of evil; it is the root of more sin, corruption, hanky-panky, and social evil than we may ever know.

Greed is an excessive, inordinate, or rapacious desire. It may be for wealth; it may be for fame; it could be a lust to excel. Some greed for power, status or ease. Others don't know what they want; they just want, want, want. These people tear down barns to build bigger ones. In the process, the greedy trample on the innocent, the hapless, the "empty"—anyone in the way. Greed often knows no bounds. Aesop created the fable of the envious, rapacious glutton to whom Zeus promised anything he wanted with one condition: his neighbor was to get a double portion. Unable to stand the thought of his neighbor faring better than himself, he asked to have one eye removed. No wonder the Lord included this command in the Decalogue—with its note of authoritative finality. Greed can transform the human personality and is capable of turning humans into beasts.

Greed is not only a blatant form of evil; it can be subtle, quite invisible and even genteel. Greed has been disguised beneath a cloak of humanitarianism. Certain entrepreneurs have muffled pangs of guilt due to excessive profits by contributing "generously" to worthy causes. Tycoons have amassed huge sums fighting union bosses who have tried to reduce the profit margin while presumably attempting to benefit the little man. So often wages lost during strikes are never made up. Professionals have often worked so long and hard amassing fortunes that there was no time for their families—no time to enjoy their fortunes. Any rosy-cheeked child would rather have more of Dad or Mom, and fewer toys. There can be greed in doing good. Greed is that subtle!

No matter where we turn we are frustrated by appeals to our greedy natures. The multiple lures to get something for nothing abound everywhere. Planned obsolescence and irreparable parts are built into more and more products (the era of repairs made with a hairpin and baling wire is past). Huge monopolies, powerful unions, automation and expanded economics all enter the domain swayed by greed. In fact, economies sometimes expand so swiftly that every available bit of humanpower is needed, resulting in many spiritually bankrupted homes. The opposite may be just as true as wives and mothers join the hurrying throng, not because of economic necessity but because of a tinge of greed. The desire for more, for better living conditions, for a few more items to ease the shrinking hours available, and desire to make education easier or better often border on covetousness and greed rather than altruism.

Greed so often snuffs out the joy of doing something for someone simply for the enjoyment of it. Johnny misses the value of shoveling Grandpa's driveway because he shovels it for the fiver, not as a favor; and Grandpa deprives Johnny's joy because he can't stand a favor without giving a fiver. It gets to be a vicious circle.

In times of affluence, greed diminishes the above sense and becomes a different kind of a problem. An affluent society finds it difficult to be satisfied with what it has; it is not necessarily jealous of what others may have and may not need another thing—in fact, it sometimes tries to give things away. Satiation is another negative side effect of covetousness.

The hippie movement is a vivid example of this. There were no poverty-stricken hippies. In order to become a true hippie, one had to renounce a comfortable status if not affluence. Their renunciation was reflected by the garb they wore, the places where they lived, the food they ate, the jobs they didn't have, the responsibilities they avoided. They were (among other things) fed up with their material blessings. Things, they said, had taken the place of people. They, in effect, were satiated but not fulfilled.

It is often true that the more you have the more you want. It is equally true, however, that often the more you have, the more difficult it is to be happy or satisfied with what you've got. This leads to getting more, going places, trying things (like drugs, fads, schools, mates) in hope of finding satisfaction somewhere, somehow, sometime. One way or another, it seems that each generation has its own hip movement protesting the way of "affluence without serenity."

Somehow, the perceptive know that something is wrong but are not quite sure what it is. Since it seemingly was caused by the preceding generation, they get the blame; and rather than run the risk of perpetuating the shortcomings of the preceding generation, it seems easier or safer to repudiate it.

This is why this tenth commandment is important. The arrangement of God's blueprint was no accident. There is no way this commandment can be fulfilled unless the other nine are given their due consideration. Elton Trueblood in his *Foundations for Reconstruction* writes with keen perception:

It is reasonable that the problem of greed should engage our attention at the end of the classic series, because greed, in its many forms, is the last enemy of both noble and ignoble minds. So great is the power of greed that we shall never overcome it wholly, as long as we are finite men. We cannot eradicate it, but we can learn to recognize it in its various disguises and find some ways of living in which the power it represents is balanced by an equal and opposite power . . .

The last sin is the most difficult sin. Just as there is a positive moral law which underlies all the specific moral laws concerning the sacredness of life, of marriage, of ownership and of veracity, so there is a temptation which underlies all other temptations, bringing all the particular aspects of the good life into constant jeopardy.

The pervasive fact of human greed constantly endangers life itself, because men will sacrifice even the lives of other men to achieve their own greedy ends; it constantly endangers the sanctity of marriage, in that unbridled lust is merely one of the forms which the love of power takes, often involving much more than mere physical desire; it constantly endangers the dignity of ownership because we covet the possessions which other men have, and therefore find subtle ways of justifying ourselves when we take them; it constantly endangers the structure of mutual trust, because greed will make us distort the truth in order to degrade our competitor or to elevate ourselves in relation to him. The sophistication of the classic formulation lies in the fact that it goes beyond the overt actions to the source of actions, and that it puts the final emphasis on the motive rather than the deed.[1]

Just as greed disrupts and distorts the truth of the previous nine commandments, these nine axioms, when upheld, make greed more difficult, if not impossible.

Since it is impossible to deal adequately with the tenth law without understanding and observing the preceding nine, let us review them briefly.

    I. PRIORITY—God demands first place in our lives and expects us to reexamine our total experience and put those highest priorities first.

    II. SUPERIORITY—God wants us to know that He has created a superior way of life (religion) for us, and does not want us to consider our faith as just another of many religious cults.

    III. SOLEMNITY—God is a holy and a just God and demands that we take Him with utmost seriousness.

    IV. FRAILTY—God knows that we are frail, fragile creatures (physically and spiritually)—consequently He created the Sabbath for us.

    V. SECURITY—The family is essential in order to

create a sense of security (belonging) and to establish a place where God's plan for the human race may unfold in the best possible atmosphere.

VI. SANCTITY—Human life is sacred; therefore, no one is to tamper with the life of another. The human body houses the soul which is eternal. Humankind is God's crowning achievement, made in His own image and likeness.

VII. FIDELITY—God has placed a high premium on marriage and its intimate personal relationships.

VIII. GENEROSITY—The generous soul is a magnanimous person; the entire economic order of the universe hangs upon this command as well.

IX. FIDELITY—Bearing false witness blights the soul. The reputation and honor of our neighbor is one of the most important things he has.

X. SERENITY—Greed plagues everyone resulting in satiation and/or covetousness. Man can only be serene when his innermost hunger has been met. This is the ultimate result of the whole law of God.

It is difficult to imagine the Ten Commandments given in an order other than what we have. Greed, as we have seen, is the obvious villain in the last command. If we were to view it only in that light, the tenth commandment would simply be another command that might well fit in elsewhere.

God is Given First Place

However, in going one step further—and caution must be taken lest one feels that the commandments have been exhausted in this book—just as there is something special about the first, there is something special about the tenth. The starting place is *Priority*: When God is given first place, other matters will fall into place. The ending likewise is special. The serenity implied in the tenth commandment is the result of the observance of the spirit and letter of the previous nine.

Of course this is true with all the commands. They are interrelated; they do address each other; they do shed light on shadows cast by their counterparts; and it has been suggested that it is wise to understand the sanctity of the human personality (sixth) before dealing with the sacredness of marriage (seventh), and so on. However, there is a marvelous finale which ought not be obscured—contentment, serenity, peace with God and our fellowmen. This is the goal of the commandments—the ultimate goal. Any disregard of any of the preceding commands jeopardizes the scope and nature of serenity. It is not possible to keep the Sabbath, honor parenthood, safeguard marriage, protect reputations, but make a livelihood exploiting others and still expect God's blessings and His gift of serenity. It hardly seems necessary to state that God's commands are not merely maxims for the wayward when they are means for a glorious culmination. God said that if people will keep His law, the results will be worth it.

The observance of any ethical system seems hardly worth the effort unless there is something better than merely behaving. If there is no hope of inner peace—no hope of an eternity spent with the author of the system—why not cheat and get rich, blackmail and get even, jettison a spouse to take another, or exploit the Sabbath? Care must be given, of course, not to make the fallacy of saying that eternal life is because of good behavior. But this should not be done at the expense of saying that the ten laws are only that—ten laws.

Rather, the ten laws are stepping-stones; they are guidelines; they are challenges; they are directions for a lost society. When they are taught, understood and observed, there is more than accomplishment: there is serenity, contentment, inner peace; peace with God and peace with our fellowmen; a wholesome sense of well-being, of self-esteem; a reason for existence . . .

Serenity, the state of being content, is the opposite of greediness and it is the counterpart of the inability to live without being content, whether with what we have or what we are. Serenity is the ultimate goal of the Ten Commandments which were designed not only to give guidelines to show the extent to which we fail, but to introduce us to the necessity that we need divine wisdom and help.

The first four commandments are God-to-man and man-to-God relationships. The fifth is a pivotal point (the centrality of the family), and the last five are man-to-man relationships. All are essential; with the magnitude of the task before us and the complexities of human existence we may have a tendency to throw up our hands in despair and say, "What's the use!!!"

No one can possibly keep the Decalogue. God never intended that we could—not as free agents with the power of choice, God-given intelligence, wisdom, conscience, and inner yearnings to communicate with the eternal Deity. Had we been created as robots, God could have easily manipulated us from His exalted position. But He chose to create us free, knowing that we would falter along the way. In His providence He also created a way of escape.

The Decalogue however, has value—strategic, critical value for the twentieth century. It is a "blueprint" of God's provision for us. The Beatitudes did not replace the law; Pauline teaching did not make the law obsolete. In fact, Jesus Himself said that He came not to destroy the law but to fulfill it. The law is a guideline, a pattern for us as individuals, as families, as nations to follow. It must be understood in the context of all of Scripture. It must be seen in relationship to the law of love, to the atonement, to the entire New Testament. Yet, no matter how we look at it, there is something explicit, exact, inclusive, unfathomable, inexhaustible and yes, contemporary. It is newer than new. When explored in depth (and we have only scratched the surface), it can bring meaning out of chaos. It will challenge the unchallenged, stimulate the passive, and encourage the crestfallen.

However, the law is not the end. This leads us to the final chapter on the fulfillment of the Decalogue—the power and stamina necessary to build the kind of a life and home outlined in God's blueprint.

FOR STUDY OR DISCUSSION

1. How do we "hunger and thirst" after righteousness? Do

many actually do this?

2. Do you agree that the tenth commandment has its greatest significance only when the other nine have been fulfilled (or at least reasonably so)? Where else could it be placed in the Decalogue?

3. How does this tenth principle cut across poverty and affluence alike?

4. Illustrate how greed negatively affects our society. Can you see it operative in family life? In the church?

5. How can there be greed in doing good?

6. Is serenity the same as tranquility? Is serenity equal to peace with God or must there also be peace with people? Can there be peace with God without peace with people? Explain.

7. What, if any, are the differences between a Christian serenity and a secular serenity? Can you give an illustration of what you mean?

8. Do you agree with Elton Trueblood that the last sin is the most difficult sin? Why or why not?

9. After the fall of mankind, did God expect us to keep the Ten Commandments? If not, why were they given?

10. What is the relationship between law and grace? Between failure and forgiveness? Between conscience and revelation? Is God's moral law contained in the Ten Commandments or does the Decalogue comprise only a part of it?

Note

1. Elton Trueblood, *Foundations for Reconstruction* (Waco, TX: Word Books, 1972).

Chapter Eleven

LAWS AND RUMORS OF LAWS

You shall love the Lord your God . . . [and] your neighbor
as yourself
Matthew 22:37,39

> He who loves his neighbor
> has fulfilled the law (Rom.
> 13:8).

The Ten Commandments as we have seen are universal principles. They go much deeper than most of us imagine; manmade laws are shallow and proliferate at an enormous rate of speed. It's been said that there are over 600 laws in the Pentateuch; by the end of the Old Testament, supposedly over 1,000 laws pertaining to the Sabbath were on the statutes. In this light it is more than amazing that, when pressed, Jesus summarized the law into two categories: the *vertical* (God to man) and *horizontal* (man to man).

"Teacher, which is the greatest commandment in the law?" Jesus responded to the lawyer's loaded question, "You shall love the Lord your God with all your heart, with all your soul, with all your mind. This is the first and the most important commandment. There is a second, very similar in importance. "You shall love your neighbor as yourself." On these two commandments depend all the laws and the prophets. Matthew 22:36-40 (paraphrased).

Here we have the two extremes—two succinct statements versus literally thousands of laws and rumors of laws. The divine economy, whether two or ten, is a monumental achievement when we consider all the laws, rules and regulations, precepts and maxims, statutes and ordinances riding on the books and floating through courts, judges' chambers, sanctuaries and libraries of the world. To attempt to force all laws and regulations (ceremonial, civil, moral) into two or ten categories may be futile, but the principles outlined are far more inclusive than one may imagine.

To drive 55 m.p.h. on U.S. highways may not be defendable as a literal corollary of the Decalogue. But if the intent is to live with the least amount of highway carnage and to forestall, hopefully, the depletion of natural resources, we may not be too far removed from the spirit of the Ten Commandments. To ban making a fire on the Sabbath which means a cold chicken dinner may not be as necessary in the era of microwaves and automated kitchen ranges as it was at the time of Caesar. But a reckless disregard of the true meaning of the Lord's Day is out of order.

Since it's been said that "a foolish consistency is the hobgoblin of little minds," it might be wise to avoid the "hobgoblinism" that threatens even the *great* law. We can easily miss the spirit, the intent of the law; we can also become so picayunish that we create laws and mini-laws that need not exist. And we can explain or defend the law in ways that are foolish.

Rabbi Herbert S. Goldstein, past president of the Union of Orthodox Jewish Congregations of America, was professor of homiletics at Yeshiva University when he wrote *Between the Lines of the Bible: A Modern Commentary on the 613 Commandments*. These orthodox laws are found in the Pentateuch beginning with commandment number one: "Birth Control" (Gen. 1:28) and concludes with command 613, to write a "Sefer Torah" (Deut. 31:19). A Sefer Torah is commanded—with prescriptions on how to do it—of every Israelite who is to write as if he were receiving the message directly from Sinai. Incidentally, to write (or rewrite) a law is not a bad idea and could help each of us sharpen our own perceptions.

Rabbi Goldstein wrote in the preface as follows:

Ever since my earliest student days I always hoped that I might be able to bring to the non-Jewish world the true meaning of the 613 Biblical Commandments . . .

Thank G-d this hope of mine is being realized in *Between the Lines of the Bible*. Toward this end I have used as the basis of my work the *Sefer Ha-Hinnuch* (The Book of Education) by Aaron Halevi of Barcelona, a Spanish Talmudist of the thirteenth century . . . .

The subject guide is revealing as it delineates the comprehensive scope of the book dealing with subjects such as adultery, birth control, capital punishment, dietary matters, ghosts and spirits, idols, intermarriage, justice, menstruation, rituals, tattooing, transvestitism, usury, vengeance, weights and measures. Another perhaps better approach might be to catalogue some of the major categories in order to show how comprehensive the law is:

Dietary Laws
Personal Hygiene
Weights and Measures
Holidays and Festivals
Tithes and Taxes
Superstitions and Taboos
Marriage and Divorce
The Role of Women
Education and Community Responsibility

The rabbi is not speaking for all Jewry but he does say something significant when he says that we would do well not only to know the commandments, but to understand their civil and moral dimensions along with the ethical, legal and religious aspects. For instance, is the prohibition against eating unclean animals a matter of health or religion, or both? Is it an ethical or civil matter? Is it a matter of time and place, or universal?

We can easily move into a hobgoblin-type of foolish consistency as we attempt to interpret or enforce the Decalogue. Rabbi Goldstein suggests that certain laws are not made specific because a husband and wife are considered one person, or a hired servant is considered a member of the family. On the other hand, usury, for example, is similar to the bite of a serpent which may not give immediate pain but can end in destruction and death. This concept alone has led to a considerable number of lesser laws covering various forms of interest (cash, buying futures, rental reductions, or even reducing the amount of the loan). It was not enough to simply outlaw usury or encourage a humanitarian practice of brotherliness. It had to be spelled out in detail.

Not unlike most of us, Professor Goldstein also had his own hobgoblins. He spelled God G-d in many instances but either he or the editor slipped up on it several times in the printed copy. (The ancient Hebrews deliberately eliminated the vowels in writing God's name so that it could not be pronounced. Therefore, the name could not be taken in vain.) He also strained considerably in pushing certain commandments, e.g., the prohibition of birth control: "Be fruitful and multiply (Gen. 1:28)." He quotes Isaiah who said that the Lord formed the earth in order to be inhabited. But couldn't this be done with some moderation? Probably. However, in order to prove his thesis, he writes about the damage done to a woman's nervous system due to limiting the size of her family. But what of those who crack up due to too many children (or not enough bread)? He argues that motherhood is woman's highest and most exalted function. But what of women whose womb is barren or whose man is ineffectual? Or those unmarried through holy vows or otherwise?

The rabbi continues to argue his case by saying that "birth control is largely responsible for the breakdown of the stability of the marriage bond due to the lack of joy and rejuvenation of spirit that children bring to the home." Is this what Genesis 1:28 is talking about? Finally, he says that "statistics prove that the *third*, *fourth*, or *fifth* child (italics mine) is apt to be best"; and even worse, the *first* or *second* (italics mine) is "most liable to inherit some of the most outstanding physical and mental defects of the parents." While this may be statistically demonstrable, most of us have had only the *first* and *second* child (statistically) and none of us have been able to begin with the *third*, *fourth* or *fifth*. Even though the Goldstein volume is valuable, it is not without its hobgoblins. We all try too hard at times.

How quickly the wisdom of a statute succumbs to distortion; whimsy, prejudice, naiveté and a failure to do necessary homework all lead to laws and rumors of laws. Spurious as well as legitimate spin-offs must be evaluated, not only on their own merit but by the laws that have been etched in stone by eternal hands. In others words, the Decalogue serves as a check-and-balance system as it polices itself. Statistics and illustrations may highlight a point but do not prove or disprove God's impeccable (flawless) and immutable (changeless) laws. We must take every precaution as we expand or limit the Decalogue.

In other words, we can take the laws too seriously; we can limit them to a particular religion or denomination; we can attempt to be all-inclusive or selective. *Caution*: Just as the orthodox Rabbi Goldstein fails to relate to all Jews, so it is possible for us to diminish or exaggerate the scope of the Decalogue. The New Testament is invaluable in interpreting and applying the laws of the Old.

When we are told to love the Lord with all our *heart, soul*, and *mind*, we get the message. It's an all-out love with no reservations. We may also wonder if there might be a systematic significance to the terms *heart, soul*, and *mind* (Mark and Luke add the word *strength*, Matt. 22:37; Mark 12:30; Luke 10:27). It no doubt has created many sermonic outlines, and rightfully so. To love with our *heart* means from the innermost of our being. To love with our *soul* means to love as easily and as naturally as we breathe. To love with our *mind* could suggest a total yielding of our intellect, but the word *mind* is not found in Deuteronomy 6:5. The word used is *might* which suggests that we love with all the strength we have.

Consequently, rather than insist upon a natural sequence of loving (emotional, volitional, intellectual), we discover that all of these terms—*heart, soul, mind, strength*—are more interrelated than distinct. The *heart* in the Hebrew and the Greek equivalent literally suggests the innermost part of a human being, the fountain seat of all thoughts, passion, desires, appetites, affections, purposes, and endeavors. It also implies that loving in this way is sincere, genuine, without pretense. Consequently, to love with all your *heart* is to love from the depth of your being with feeling, will, and intellect.

We smile at the suitor who told his sweetheart that his love was endless, wider than the horizon, deeper than the deepest sea—and then added, "I'll be over to see you Saturday night if it doesn't rain." That's precisely the kind of love that doesn't come from the heart.

If this love is also to come from the *soul*, could there be another dimension? The word for *soul* comes from the primary root *to breathe* and changes considerably depending on the context and its prefix or suffix (ranging from "a vital principle" to a "sweet odor exhaled"). If the *heart* is the source of life, the circulatory system, the source of the senses, affections, and emotions of the mind, the *soul* is the breath of life, the result of the work, physically and spiritually, of the heart. The similarities, it appears, are far closer than the differences, and suggest a love which involves the whole being, its feelings, desires, and affections.

Added to this is the expression *mind* or *might* (or the N.T. word *strength*). The implication is a love of the highest degree, with power and strength. When the root of this word takes on a prefix or a suffix it shows its unique flavor: wholly, diligently, utterly, passionately, and even vehemently. When Mark added the word *strength* to the word *mind* (Mark 12:30), he had the same idea as Luke (10:27). This love had to be understood as a powerful, unfading, overt, aggressive, dynamic relationship. It had to involve the entire being—body, soul, and mind. It had to involve the will as well as the intellect, the emotions as well as the motives. This all-encompassing love does not miss a thing. It is total love or it isn't love at all. This must be understood when we speak about loving God with our whole being and our neighbor as ourselves. But just how do we love in this way?

This kind of total love is impossible we say. We all love and we love differently. We love our children differently than we love our spouses. We love our homes with another kind of love. We even love ice cream and sailboats; we love books and flowers; and we love the feel of soft sand on a warm evening, and a crackling fire on a December hearth. Of course, these kinds of love are not all love. Technically, we can't love ice cream or flowers, but the expression does tell us how loosely we use the word *love*.

If we are to *love* the Lord with everything we are, what do we mean by *love*? In both instances, the Old Testament and the New Testament words are consistent. The Hebrew word used for love is *'âhab* which means to have affection for, sexually or otherwise. In other words, it's a strong, general word for love. But how do we love God? Implied in this word is not only affection and high esteem, but a grateful recognition of the benefits we've received, an affectionate reverence. By loving the Lord, we are holding Him in high esteem, grateful for what He has done for us. That we can and ought to do. It is not asking the impossible.

The New Testament writers, Matthew, Mark, and Luke, all used the same word: *agapaō*. This love is a special kind of love and much has been written about it. When it refers to God's love for us, it denotes a very special relationship. When it refers to our love for others, it also is a special kind of love. This kind of love is not self-generating; it is God-given. It differs from brotherly love and the passionate reciprocity known by lovers. In other words, the capacity to love the Lord ultimately comes from the Lord Himself. When other love fades or dies, this love lives on. It loves the unlovable and loves even when love is not returned.

However, if this *agapaō* concept was unknown to the Hebrews, why was it chosen when *phileō* (brotherly affections) is actually closer to the Hebrew? That is difficult to answer except to acknowledge the depth and breadth of the word *agapaō*. Even so, the Deuteronomy word gives an important dimension which must not be overlooked. The Lord wants us to revere Him as a dear friend, a brother (as well as father). It means to desire, to breathe after something—a longing for someone. If there is no longing for God, there will be no affection, no love, no desire, no gratitude. In fact, this Hebrew expression stresses the reciprocity sometimes overlooked in its Greek equivalent. We are told to love the Lord our God as He loves us.

This can be seen in the glorious, wholesome relationship between Jonathan and David: "He loved him as he loved his own soul" (1 Sam. 20:17). The brotherly love between David and Jonathan was reciprocal as Jonathan made David verbalize his love for him. We love as we are loved.

During my college days I became acquainted with a fellow student and we became closer than brothers. Today, with the gay community coming alive (it has always been in existence but without as much notoriety), it is regrettable that this kind of brotherly love cannot exist without suspicion. I can honestly attest that in our relationship there was never the slightest sexual attraction, but there was a David-Jonathan camaraderie, a loyalty, an understanding that nearly defies description. I'd never experienced it before, nor since. We have both long since traveled different paths, and when he married I spirited the couple away to their secret honeymoon hideaway. He chose his mate well, and I couldn't have been more pleased.

This Hebrew concept of *love* is necessary. Unless we revere the Lord as a dear friend, and accentuate this with loyalty and gratitude, our love is less than it ought to be; God's law is less meaningful than it should be.

If Christ came not to destroy the law (or make it obsolete) but to fulfill it, He must have had a high regard for the law. He fulfilled it by showing that it could be kept. He who knew no sin never transgressed the Ten Commandments, an incredible achievement because even the Son of God was tempted as we are. He was tempted to say something inappropriate at several times in His earthly ministry, but He didn't. In fact, at one time he called Peter *Satan* and He nailed the Pharisees with *you whitewashed sepulchers*. It doesn't appear that He smiled as He drove the money changers out of the Temple courtyard, and when He sent Judas on his betrayal mission He didn't say what some of us might have been tempted to say.

When Satan took Him to the pinnacle of the Temple and told Him to jump, Jesus refused to buy that kind of publicity stunt and He turned down his offer to share the wealth of the Holy Land. When the disciples were thickheaded, Jesus sinned not, nor did He sin when His privacy was invaded or when 90 percent of the cleansed lepers never said as much as "Thanks." When the soldiers mocked Him and drove those spikes into His limbs, He never cursed either God or them. Rather, He prayed, "Father, forgive them . . . " Jesus lived up to both the spirit and the letter of the law.

Without the law, there is no guideline; there is no challenge; there is no temptation possible. Anything could go. Everything would be right in the eyes of the beholder. Besides, the impossibility of keeping the law could lead to frustration and eventual disillusionment. Jesus, however, has never asked us to do what He wouldn't do or go where He wouldn't go or be what He wouldn't be. When He lived and observed the moral laws of the universe in their entirety He could with clear conscience say, "Go and do likewise."

Of course, for us keeping the law is an impossibility. No human has ever done it; but that's the wonder of it all. The challenge is there. The objectives have never changed from one generation to the next. How long ago was it said that no one could run the mile in fewer than four minutes or the 100-yard dash in ten seconds? Both marks have been shattered but the world still awaits the eight-second dash and a 3:30 mile. The challenge is there, and without it, track meets could be pretty dull. So is life without a challenge. Just because we can't fulfill the demands of the Decalogue doesn't mean that the law has no value. To the contrary, finding it such a challenge is good news, not bad. What most of us need is not a new set of rules but a challenge to rediscover the ones that exist.

Paul was struggling with many aspects of the Christian life

in Romans 13. His struggle included subjection to governing authorities and living with our conscience. He pleads with Christians today as well as he reminds us to give respect to whom respect is due and honor to whom honor is due. While finished with his admonition to maintain proper respect for governing officials (and those in power at the time of Paul were hardly benevolent), Paul changes the subject. Or does he?

Of the many obligations we have, there is one Paul insists we must not overlook:

> Love one another; for he who loves his neighbor has fulfilled the law. The commandments, "You shall not commit adultery, You shall not kill, You shall not steal, You shall not covet," and any other commandment, are summed up in this sentence: "You shall love your neighbor as yourself." Love does no wrong to a neighbor; therefore love is the fulfilling of the law (Rom. 13:8-10).

Paul amplified this love when he wrote to the Christians at Corinth. Again, it's impossible to live in perfect fulfillment of the law but what a challenge it is—and that's the marvel of the Christian faith. It is challenging, it is demanding, it is explicit.

Since God is love and Jesus and God are one, it follows that Jesus is love. If we who are believers—parents, pastors and teachers, children and adults, neighbors—we are to be as Christlike as possible. What better guideline is there than the spirit of the thirteenth chapter of 1 Corinthians?

A Christian is very patient and kind, never jealous or envious, never boastful or proud, never haughty nor selfish nor rude. A believing parent does not demand his or her way. He or she is not irritable or touchy and does not hold grudges or gloat over the misfortunes of others.

A Christian is a neighbor who is loyal no matter what the cost, gives the benefit of a doubt; is ready to give a helping hand and doesn't give up easily (paraphrased).

At times we believers, parents and children, citizens and neighbors are novices. We don't always behave wisely or with maturity. We may possess, on the other hand, a keen intellect and specialized gifts. We may even have unusual perception and insights. But these will all fade along with our frailties and imperfections. The only lasting power in life, the home, and the neighborhood is love.

For God so loved the world that He gave His only begotten son the author and perfecter of our faith that whosoever loves God with his whole heart and soul and his neighbor as himself shall not perish but have life abundant not only now but in the life to come.

If the Ten Commandments are understood and practiced as God's moral and ethical law, and faith in Christ Jesus is essential for salvation, where could this be taught more effectively and efficiently than in the home? A home could be an extended family of parents and grandparents with cousins and nephews, uncles, and aunts living under the same roof. A home could be a single parent living with a child or two . . . Home could be a modest room in a faraway mansion where Gram and Gramps take turns praying for their beloved family. Or a home could be Mom and Dad and their children . . .

The family is God's gift to the earth, the home is God's gift to the family. May the Lord grant unto each of us wisdom and desire to build according to the plan He has carved with love in stone.

FOR STUDY OR DISCUSSION

1. Are the Ten Commandments universal or mainly Judeo-Christian principles? Is human nature basically the same everywhere even though conditioned by local mores and ethics, etc.?
2. Why was this chapter titled, "Laws and Rumors of Laws"?
3. What is meant by "hobgoblinism"? Does it threaten the Great Law? What is the Great Law?
4. Do the biblical commandments encompass virtually every aspect of human existence (e.g. dietary laws, personal hygiene, tithes and taxes, marriage and divorce,

roles of women and children, community responsibility, etc.)? Do the principles if not the specific laws cover all human existence?

5. Discuss the various aspects of love (e.g. charitable, brotherly, erotic, friendship, fondness, liking, passionate, etc.). Which of these are closest to the love with which we should love the Lord our God?

6. What does it mean to love the Lord God with all our heart, soul, and might?

7. What does it mean to love our neighbor as we love ourselves? Should a Christian who diligently follows the Ten Commandments possess a high degree of self-esteem?

8. Does the David-Jonathan relationship (closer than brothers) help us in understanding our relationship to the Lord?

9. Describe how Jesus fulfilled the law as He lived His life on earth.

10. How do you explain: "He who loves his neighbor has fulfilled the law"?

EPILOGUE

Luke 10:25-37

One day when Jesus had irritated the religious leaders, they plotted how they might reduce His effectiveness. After plotting their strategy, a brilliant professor was dispatched to argue with Jesus, hoping to embarrass Him publicly. The professor waited for the opportune moment. When it came he stood up to put Jesus into His proper place. "Rabbi," he said courteously, "what must I do to inherit eternal life?"

The crowd held its breath realizing that a showdown was near. Jesus paused a moment and then tossed the ball back into the professor's court. "Sir, you know the ancient law extremely well. How do you interpret it?" Now the professor was on the spot. Jesus had answered a question with a question, a remarkable strategy reminding us of the proverbial exchange, "Why do you Jews always answer a question with a question?" "Why shouldn't we?"

The lawyer knew his law. Quickly he answered quoting verbatim from the ancient manuscripts, "You shall love the Lord your God with all your heart, and with all your soul, and with all your strength, and with all your mind; and your neighbor as yourself" (Luke 10:27).

Jesus nodded His approval and ended the conversation, "You have answered right; do this and you will have eternal life." But the professor, not seeking an honest answer, was totally unprepared for what was to follow. In a moment of smug confidence, he delivered what he had hoped would be the decisive word, "And who is my neighbor?"

Jesus took the blow without flinching. Accepting the challenge, He struck back with one of His incredible parables:

A man was going down from Jerusalem to Jericho when he was ambushed by a band of bandits. They jumped him as he rounded the bend, stripped him of everything, even his clothes, and left him half dead. Cowards they were. They took off before a solitary figure came upon the scene traveling in the same direction as the victim. He, of all who should have given assistance, sized up the situation, shrugged his shoulders and passed by.

The priest may have been in a hurry (many of the Temple priests lived in Jericho we're told) or possibly he didn't care to touch a dead man's body if he assumed that he was not alive. Shortly after this a Levite came by. He too would be expected to give a man a helping hand, but for some reason he passed by on the other side.

Then came a traveler, a man considered least likely to give assistance. He was a Samaritan, and although Jesus doesn't say so, the victim no doubt was a Jew. Immediately the Samaritan sized up the situation, administered aid, placed the half-dead man on his own donkey and brought him to the nearest inn. He gave instructions to the innkeeper to nurse this man back to health. Before continuing on his way he paid the innkeeper in advance and guaranteed all expenses.

By now the crowd was deathly silent. Jesus had won: "Which of these three, in your opinion, was a neighbor to the man who had fallen victim to the robbers?" What else could the lawyer say? "The one who showed mercy." Then Jesus ended the conversation,

"Go and do likewise" (paraphrased).

The Samaritans and the Jews despised each other. The contrast was awesome—a religious man would be expected to give aid, the Samaritan would not, especially if the injured man was a Jew. The audience couldn't miss the point. But it didn't end there. The good neighbor went beyond the call of duty. He risked his own life. He soiled his own garments lifting the beaten stranger onto the back of his beast. He spent his own money caring for the one in desperate need. He paid in advance and promised the innkeeper-turned-physician adequate reimbursement for any future expense. And he said he'd come by when his journey was over to see how everything was going.

The moral of the story is obvious. We should love our neighbor who may be a total stranger, even a despised member of society, as though he were a son or a dear friend. Even more than that, we should do naturally what others wouldn't do, naturally or otherwise. Would the professor with whom Jesus was debating have given aid? Probably not. He probably wouldn't have even lent a helping hand to a fellow professor—and he knew it. So did the crowd.

Now we know a little more about neighbors and being neighborly, don't we? If we don't love our neighbor, is it possible to love the Lord our God? Or should we turn that around? If we don't love the Lord our God, is it possible to love our neighbor?